FINDING THE KEY TO PERSONAL INTEGRITY

FINDING THE KEY TO PERSONAL INTEGRITY

MARY PYTCHES

Arcadia

Bath, England

DEDICATION

Not many women have the good fortune to be married
for forty-five years to a man who is fun, encouraging and
stimulating. I have had that privilege and I would like to
dedicate this book to him.

To my husband David – a man of integrity.

Copyright © 2002 by Mary Pytches.
Published by Arcadia Publishing Services Ltd, Reverie, Keels Hill, Peasdown
St John, Bath BA2 8EW.

British Library Cataloguing in Publication Data. A catalogue record for this
book is available from the British Library.

Scripture quotations unless otherwise noted are from *The Holy Bible*, New
International Version, Copyright © 1973, 1978, 1984 by International Bible
Society. Used by permission of Hodder & Stoughton, a Division of Hodder
Headline.

Typeset by Arcadia Publishing Services Ltd
Printed by Cox & Wyman, Reading
ISBN No: 0-86347-503-5 (Eagle)
ISBN No: 1-904404-02-2 (Arcadia)

CONTENTS

INTRODUCTION

'You hypocrite, first take the plank out of your own eye, and then you will see clearly to remove the speck from your brother's eye.'[1] Jesus never minced his words and those frank comments have made me hesitate to put pen to paper on the subject of self-awareness and integrity. Despite my fears of opening myself to the accusation of hypocrisy, I have embarked on the task of tackling a subject that has been in my thinking for a long time, and I believe is particularly relevant in this post-modern era.

Obviously writing on the theme of integrity I have been compelled to search my own heart in the process. To say I had reached the place of total integrity myself would be untrue but as I doubt that this side of heaven I will, I didn't feel I could wait until I had arrived to write this book!

I am not the only one to have the feeling that integrity is being eroded in our present society. In Os Guinness's excellent book, *A Time for Truth*, he highlights today's crisis of truth and demonstrates that living in the truth has very real consequences in every sphere of life. The challenge has made me question, given our present culture, how it would be possible to become a person of the truth. When I look in the mirror I become aware of the blemishes on my face, or the smudges under my eyes, or the clash in my colour scheme. Only as I am made aware of the flaws can I put them right. *Finding the Key to Personal Integrity* is a book about self-awareness that I believe is the key to integrity.

As always I have to thank my husband David for his painstaking reading and editing of the manuscript. I am amazed that he has the patience. Not only does he correct my grammar, but he even goes the second mile and searches his books and newspapers for illustrations and quotes for me. I can only think that he truly loves me!

Chapter One

TRUTH ENDANGERED

'They are not of the world, even as I am not of it. Sanctify them by the truth; your word is truth.'
(Jn. 17:16–17)

I became a Christian in 1954. I had come from a God-fearing, though non-church attending family and they had drummed into me the importance of leading a moral life. Honesty was expected and generally I was happy to accept their standards. It was not until my late teens that I began to doubt the existence of God. I could find no proof that he existed and if he did, that he was interested in me. But in 1954 I was invited to a guest service at a nearby church. The service was quiet and dignified, and the preaching very convincing. I started to think that perhaps Christianity had something to offer me after all. Week by week I listened to well reasoned sermons. The logical arguments I heard convinced me and I finally made a decision to become a Christian. I was sure that I had found the piece that was missing in my life and took up my discipleship with enthusiasm. I signed up for a course called 'School for Christians', which fed me doctrine in digestible mouthfuls. I went to Bible College and received some more well-thought out and rational teaching on the Christian faith. I learned the four spiritual laws that were designed to persuade non-believers of the validity of the faith. I read books like *Who moved the Stone?* that convinced me by the sheer power of its arguments that Christ had risen from the dead and must be the Son of God.

Forty years later, I found myself having a meal with a group of black-clad, Gothic style, body-pierced young people. They were a very spiritual bunch, and yet their language confused me. They were religious and yet worryingly inclusive. Yes, they believed in Jesus, but were also learning from other religions. According to them they lived moral lives and yet they were uncritical of those that chose to live in lifestyles which were diametrically opposed to Biblical standards. There appeared to be no moral absolutes for them. They expressed a tolerance for everything, except my belief in the existence of objective truth. Talking to them was like trying to grasp a bar of slippery soap in the bath.

During the forty years between my conversion to Christ and that conversation there has been a monumental shift in Western culture. The West has moved from the safe, rational, world view, which I had inherited as a young Christian, with its objective truth, to a post-modern culture with no absolutes. The old arguments fail to impress the new generation.

This massive shift in the western world view affects us in many different ways. But none more than in the area of truth, which in turn has lead to a crisis of integrity. However, before considering the vital importance of integrity we need to understand the roots of the present post-modern culture.

POSTWAR HOPEFULNESS

The world I grew up in was one of hope and confidence. The two world wars were over – world peace seemed assured. Scientific discovery held out exciting new prospects for health, education, travel and the possibility of penetrating the ultimate mysteries of the universe in which we lived. It seemed that we were near to finding answers to the fundamental questions of life, while our new technology was racing ahead and opening doors to major scientific discov-

eries and enormous economic growth. We could imagine a
Utopian reality, where disease, poverty, and ignorance were
things of the past. The two writers, Middleton and Walsh
called this the culture of confidence. We saw ourselves as the
masters of our own destiny and the world.[1]

THE ONSET OF POST-MODERNITY

However, as the twentieth century progressed confidence
began to wane. The myth of progress was losing its power.
'These days it sounds like a fairy tale too good to be true.'[2]
Those hopes of modernity had rested upon the shoulders of
fallible humanity. There had been something unrealistic
about it. We were not made to be 'homo autonomous' – to
go it alone. Our progress had given rise to disillusionment,
to a sense of hopelessness and a turning away from the con-
fident beliefs of the self-assured, self-centred society we lived
in. This could be seen in the General Election of 2001 when
a worrying percentage of the population had not even bothered to vote. They were too cynical – they no longer
believed in the hype and spin of the politicians. Another
disconcerting feature of Western society is the number of
angry and violent protests being staged against globalisation,
the cartels and the conglomerates perceived to be running the
world. Despair has been giving rise to frustration with the
system. The promised Utopia was not just round the corner
after all.

   When we lived in South America we suffered frequent
earthquakes. Often the big one was preceded by smaller
quakes and then followed by after shocks. The problem was
to determine where we actually were in the process. Were
we working up to the big one, or had we had it? Was there
a bigger one to come, or was the earth just settling down
again? In the same way no one knows where we are in this
cultural shift. Has it arrived or are we still on the journey.
Hence the lack of a name. It's just post the last era – post-
modernism – the name given to it until we find a better one.

But, as with an earthquake, it leaves the population in a state of uncertainty. Our whole culture seems to have the willies. Many intelligent, high-powered, well-educated people seem unable to make the ordinary decisions of living, such as entering into committed relationships and having children.[3]

THE DEATH OF TRUTH

Another serious consequence of this disillusionment and despair is the death of truth as we have known it. Truth in any objective or absolute sense, truth that is independent of the mind of the knower, no longer exists apparently. At best, it is relative – it's a matter of interpretation and all depends on one's perspective. At worst, truth is 'socially constructed' – merely a matter of human convention.[4]

The Monica Lewinsky trial in America illustrates this worrying feature of our society when Bill Clinton assured the American public on National Television 'I did not have sexual relations with that woman.' That was his interpretation of the truth – the truth as he wanted to present it and others to believe it. But when the nature of his misconduct came to light, most normal people would have considered his involvement as an extremely intimate form of sexual activity. Bill Clinton played with words to make something seem true that apparently was untrue. A classic statement he made at the time was: 'It depends what the meaning of "is" is.'

That illustrates post-modernism!

Os Guinness makes the point that Clinton was the first president in the post-modern era, and the first president to be post-modern through and through. He says that the Lewinsky affair was an excellent gauge by which to assess the impact of post-modernism on American politics and law. In terms of the standing of truth in the American republic, the scandal represents the post-modern crisis of truth in presidential form. As he says, it was the year America learned to live with the lie.[5] So at home were the American people with his lies that even after such a blatant challenge to his integrity 60%+ of them were prepared to back his presidency, because they believed he was doing a good job with the economy. The cheating on his wife, the lack of personal discipline and the lies were relatively unimportant. The public were inured to any lack of integrity. This attitude of lying was encapsulated on a bumper sticker. 'President Clinton, 99% Fact-Free!'[6] The public seemed to be shrugging their shoulders and saying to themselves: 'Well, that's just the way he is!' But similar stories could be told of many public figures across the world.

Few seem to believe any longer in the sort of objective truth which gave me such confidence as a young Christian, and still keeps me going today. Truth has been so strangely tampered with, that the modern mind is left in a state of confusion. Truth today has become something subjective. If it's your truth then it is as valid as someone else's truth. It all depends on how you see it and from what angle you are viewing it. We could call it truth decay!

David and I have been growing an orchid for two years. We are immensely proud of our achievement and every now and again count the blooms. One morning, sitting at our breakfast table we had a mild argument as to the number of flowers on the stem. I said there were six. David said there were seven. Well he was right. There were seven flowering, though from where I was sitting I could only see six. We both spoke the truth as we saw it because our conclusions depended on our perspective. We could have left the argument at six and seven. After all, in the present cultural climate, I am permitted to enjoy my truth and he is permitted his. But in fact we are both still modernist at heart who like to get to the bottom of things and try to be objective. So we concluded the truth was that there were seven flowering already and there were three buds yet to open.

A story which I have heard and has appeared in several books, illustrates this post-modern view of truth. Three cricket umpires were debating their different philosophies of umpiring. The first one declared that there are 'no-balls and there's wides, and I call them the way they are'. 'That's arrogant,' declared the second. 'There's no-balls and there's wides, and I call them the way I see it.' 'Why not be realistic about what we do,' said the third. 'There's no-balls and there's wides and they are nothing until I call them.'[7] The first umpire represents the modernist view of truth. It is objective and there to be discovered. The second umpire is a moderate post-modernist. In his case truth is what each person perceives it to be. This is probably the most commonly held post-modern position. The third umpire, however, takes a radical post-modern view of truth. For him truth is for each of us to create for ourselves. This is an even more worrying stance.

THE INSIDIOUS NATURE OF CULTURE

When we first went to South America our introduction to the new culture was much more of a shock to the system than we had ever imagined. We walked down the gangway from our air-conditioned cabin out into a noisy, baking hot harbour with a host of unfamiliar shouts from waiting families full of extraordinary emotion, and the garlic breath of busy porters passing by. Our new environment hit us in the face. Adjustments were difficult at first. But after a while we became acclimatised. For example, we would invite people to our meetings and they would respond most politely. 'Thank you, we will do all that is possible to come.' Clearly we could expect quite a crowd and we would arrange more chairs in eager anticipation. It took months of disappointment to realise that a blunt: 'No' for a Chilean was considered extremely rude. Their way of excusing themselves politely was to say they'd do all they could to try and make it, which everyone but ourselves understood to mean, 'Sorry I don't think we'll be coming.' On one occasion we invited a Chilean family to tea. We expected them at four o'clock, so

I set the table and laid out the sandwiches, a cake and some biscuits in anticipation. Four o'clock came and went. By five we were giving up, when there was a ring at the front door bell. We rushed to the door only to find some American friends who were just dropping by to say, 'Hi'. We invited them in and suggested they share the tea we had prepared. They tucked into the tea and were just finishing when the door bell went again. It was six o'clock. The Americans left by the back door as our Chilean guests came in very belatedly at the front. Greatly embarrassed I had to prepare more sandwiches and do my best with the leftover cake and biscuits. I have never forgotten it because these Chileans invited us back later to a huge banquet in our honour! Punctuality was not a priority in their cultural agenda, but generous hospitality was.

Cultural differences were immediately noticeable though it took us some time to become used to it. The cultural changes we face in the West today are much more insidious. What is happening may not be very obvious to most of us, though sociologists and those directly involved with the younger generation, are still busy trying to analyse it. Nevertheless it is all around us and like it or not we are partakers of it. It is like being in the same room as a cigarette smoker. We may not be smoking ourselves but we are breathing in the fumes. Whatever our age or beliefs the culture has an effect upon us. We may even be changed by it without realising it. And that's a dangerous position to be in.

The attitude to truth is not the only thing that has changed. There are other more obvious trends. Sexuality, the drug culture and family life are some examples. It is easy to bury our heads and pretend nothing is wrong when young people are dying from Aids. The homeless and the drug addicts sleep rough on our high streets. Families readily split apart. Fathers are conspicuous by their absence. One-parent families abound, and our babies are reared by strangers. The walls of modernity are crumbling, and comfortable, educated, well-to-do Westerners tuck themselves into their warm houses and deny what is happening.[8] There is a crisis going on that we cannot afford to ignore.

However it is the crisis of truth that most concerns us here.

THE IMPORTANCE OF TRUTH

We ignore the present trend at our peril because 'truth is one of the simplest, most precious gifts without which we would be unable to handle reality or negotiate life,' writes Os Guinness. 'Neither unhealthy nor repressive, truth is a vital requirement not only for individuals who would live a good life but for free societies that would remain free.'[9] Part of the post-modern despair is to do with the empty promises of the spin doctors, the insincere smiles which we don't trust any longer, the pronouncements from powerful leaders which turn out to be lies in disguise. How can society hope to survive in a world with such deception?

Lying in all its forms is a danger to freedom. Only 'the truth will set you free,' said Jesus.[10] Lying leads to more lying, whether in public or private, and we gradually become trapped in a web of deceit. When lying is the norm how can we trust anyone any longer. We cannot relate to those we cannot believe. The soap opera, *EastEnders* is a very popular programme especially among young people. But nearly all the characters in it lie regularly – in every episode someone is saving face, covering up infidelity, or extorting money by lying. It was said on television in the USA recently that the average American lied 25 times a day! No one can be trusted. The young accept that as the norm. What are they learning? That lying is OK, but trusting people is not a good idea!

CHRISTIAN INTEGRITY

There is nothing new about lying, or playing with truth.

The truth has been under attack since the beginning of time. Satan tempted Adam and Eve with a lie contradicting God's word to them. God had said that if they ate from the tree of the knowledge of good and evil that they would surely die. Satan said, 'You will not surely die.'[11]

When Jesus came into the world he claimed he was the way the *truth* and the life.[12] Later he said to Pilate that he had come into the world to testify to the truth and that everyone on the side of truth listened to him.[13] Pilate replied with a question that made him sound like a post-modernist. 'What is truth?' he asked.

So the loss of sincerity and truthfulness are not new phenomena but what post-modernism has done is to give the world an excuse to reject those precious assets too easily. Integrity should be a high priority for the Christian. Yet we can be as much affected by the new cultural laxity as anyone else. In one week, recently, I heard of three Christian leaders who had been caught in gross misconduct. All three caused great grief and pain to the people close to them, but were evidently more concerned about their own satisfaction and happiness, than the feelings of others. A church member said to her pastor, when faced with the effect of her adultery on her children: 'This isn't about them. It's about me and my happiness.' For Christians to hurt those who depend upon them there has to be an avoidance of the truth; truth about other people's feelings; truth about their own responsibility; truth about commitment to Christian standards of morality. When such things happen even the world looks on and shakes its head at the hypocrisy.

Just the other day an invitation came through the post addressed to my husband. It was headed 'A very private, personal, invitation from the Office of the President' (of some Christian organisation). I was impressed! But as I read on I was appalled by the complete lack of integrity in the letter. The person addressed David by his Christian name as if he knew him intimately and then proceeded to call him a treasured member of our spiritual family. This man said that he honestly believed that David was marked for God's spiritual blessings. David had never met this man in his life, though the letter was purported to be addressed only to the closest members of his spiritual family. We are accustomed to receiving these sort of con-letters from worldly organisations who want us to believe we have won some enormous sum of money, but not from a Christian leader. But this is the danger we all face. We live in the world and it's easy to be sucked into its practices, and into believing that the end justifies the means.

We need to warn one another that just as carbon monoxide poisoning gradually kills, so will the prevailing culture of the lie, unless we speak the truth to each other (in love) and learn to let our 'Yes', be 'Yes' and our 'No', 'No'.[14] We have a unique opportunity to live radically different lives today and become marked for being people of real integrity. It's time to draw on and fasten the belt of truth and stand against the enemy, who is the 'Father of Lies'. As Christians 'our overarching life-task will be clear: to seek the truth, speak the truth and live the truth.'[15] If this is our goal the next question is how? How can we be full participators in our society and still maintain our integrity?

Chapter Two

SELF-AWARENESS

'Three things are extremely hard – steel, diamonds and knowing oneself.'
(Benjamin Franklin)

Integrity is in short supply in every walk of life. Pick up any newspaper and 'read all about it'. In business life, in political life and in personal life, we are more concerned with image, power, success and money than with integrity. Even as Christians it is only too easy to be sucked into the prevailing attitude without even realising what is happening to us. The prophet Jeremiah tells us bluntly that 'The heart is deceitful above all things and beyond cure. Who can understand it?'[1] Given this inclination to self-deception how can we make sure we don't slide down the same slippery slope as everyone else? 'For self-deception, by its very nature, is the most elusive of mental facts. We do not see what it is that we do not see.'[2]

Such deception, in some cases, could lead to monumental disasters. We live in a dangerous era. After September 11th and the bombing by terrorists of the twin towers in New York, the world may never feel totally safe again. We face threats unknown in other times. Sudden death from nuclear war, or the gradual breakdown of our ecology is a distinct possibility. Whether the end comes quickly or slowly, 'the human capacity for self-deception will have played its part.'[3] This collective capacity for self-deception could lead us to a world disaster, or endangering smaller groups of people. Over the years a variety of cults have appeared on the scene, and at the time we have all wondered how a group of people could be so hoodwinked. One such scandal to hit the English scene was the Sheffield Nine O'clock Service that ended in total disillusionment for some 200, or more, young people. When it was over many of them claimed not to understand how they could have been so easily conned and manipulated by Chris Brain, the group leader. But self-deception operates both at the level of the individual mind, and in the collective awareness of a group. To belong to a group of any sort, the tacit price of membership is usually to overlook personal feelings of uneasiness and misgiving, and certainly never to challenge the group's way of doing things.[4] Dissent, even healthy dissent, is always stifled.

More commonly our self-deception leads to some sort of personal disaster, though to some degree, it always affects others. The story of the Assemblies of God Pastor, Richard Dortch, was a very salutary one. In 1983 he was invited by Jimmy and Tammy Bakker to become the executive director of Heritage USA, a huge Christian enterprise, very familiar on American television. Dortch was a man with a reputation for integrity. People relaxed knowing he was now in control of the enormous and complex organisation. Heritage was a 2,300-acre site, situated in North Carolina, which had its own utilities, shops, restaurants, campground, recreational complex, and television studio and network. It offered many contemporary and fashionable homes on site for sale. It was an exciting project. Then in 1988 Richard Dortch, this man of integrity, was arrested and indicted for fraud. Though he did not intentionally defraud the public, nevertheless he was the man responsible for Heritage USA at the time. With hindsight he said that he had lost his sensitivity because of arrogance. People had told him over and over that nothing could go wrong with him there, and he believed them. He deceived himself into believing that he was above it all. 'I became so intoxicated with the growth of Heritage USA, so enamoured with what was developing around me that I refused to see what was happening; the sins of adultery, fornication, embezzlement, etc.'[5] He had become selective about what he noticed and what he did not. His overlooking of glaring irregularities led to personal disaster, pain for his family and public disgrace.

Daniel Goleman talks about the 'narcotic of self-deception.'[6]

THE ANTIDOTE OF SELF-AWARENESS

The most effective antidote to self-deception is self-awareness – to know oneself. In fact King David called out to God to help him to do this. He cried: 'Search me, O God, and know my heart; test my thoughts. Point out anything you find in me that makes you sad, and lead me along the path of everlasting life.'[7] David knew how important self-awareness was and he knew how difficult it was to keep working at it. Sadly most of us are not given to regular self-examination. We tend to live our lives doing whatever comes to hand without giving it much thought, and we often contravene our own standards in the process. Without self-knowledge we are in constant danger of deceiving and hurting ourselves and others.

A loss of integrity can happen to almost anyone. It occurs because we have a natural bias toward the self, which causes us, often unconsciously, to put our own interests first. So if it makes us look good or feel good; if it gives us a buzz, or protects our sensitive feelings, then we will do anything or say anything, without a backward glance, unless, somewhere along the line, we have developed the practice of asking ourselves some difficult questions. It is a hard pill to swallow to realise that even the good we do can have within it a mixture of self-interest and self-sacrifice at the same time. For example I have had many people come to see me suffering from burnout. They claimed to be exhausted from helping out, serving others and organising people. They

seemed unable to say 'no' to any request for help. These
people are so self-sacrificing, and yet there must be something wrong for them to have become so exhausted.

The key was usually motivation. We all need to stop
now and again and ask ourselves the question: 'Why am I
doing what I am doing?' At first the answer will usually be
the obvious one. 'I love to help others, and I have always
been a helper.' But if we look a little deeper and probe a little harder there is usually a hidden motive. With one young
man it was a need to calm down any situation which looked
as if it was becoming chaotic. His father had been an alcoholic and as a child his life had been fraught with anxiety.
He was constantly trying to protect his mother and calm his
drunken father. As an adult that same childhood anxiety
would rise up and swamp him whenever a situation looked
as if it was getting out of hand, unless he could be actively
involved in bringing some order to the situation. Another
person would respond positively to every request for help,
even when she knew her diary was already overbooked. She
never stopped to ask herself if it was right to say 'yes'. She
usually agreed to requests immediately without pausing to
think. Her quick reaction was her way of protecting herself
from discomfort. She disliked appearing to reject anyone.
She was acutely aware of what it felt like. Though she knew
she should say 'no', her fear of seeing her own pain reflect-
ed in another person's face overruled her common sense.

Becoming self-aware people does not mean we will
immediately stop doing senseless things. But asking questions of ourselves will act as a brake upon us. The knowing
leads us on to the next step, which is asking God to heal and
transform us. We are all still on a journey towards healing
and wholeness. No one has yet arrived. But at least there is
honesty in admitting one's true state. It's fine to run an
obstacle race blindfolded if those are the rules, but it's stupid if it is meant to be run with one's eyes wide open.
Christians are encouraged to 'walk in the light, as he [Jesus]

is in the light.' In this way we can have fellowship with one another.[8] It is hard to be in the company of someone who lacks self-knowledge. Such a person can be very hurtful and quite unaware of the effect s/he is having upon others. Only the other day I heard of a young woman who has a very prickly, even angry manner. She leaves her victims devastated, but doesn't seem to notice the effect she has upon them. When I suggested that someone should draw her attention to her behaviour, I was told no one was brave enough. I felt sorry for the poor woman who will soon find herself friendless, unless she has the courage to examine herself and ask herself some really hard questions.

WHAT SELF-AWARENESS IS NOT

In promoting self-awareness I am not talking about self-absorption. It's amazing how negatively some people will react when asked to become more self-conscious – or more self-aware. Scott Peck's book, *People of the Lie*, is a shocking book about people who, at all costs, avoid any self-scrutiny, and therefore any self-criticisms. One of the stories concerns a young man called Bobby, who was admitted to hospital suffering from depression. Bobby's older brother had committed suicide, shooting himself with a gun given him by his parents, and though, at first, Bobby had coped with the loss fairly well he had subsequently become depressed and uncommunicative. While trying to get to the bottom of Bobby's problems, Scott Peck was amazed to discover that Bobby had been given his brother's gun as a Christmas present, even though he had asked for a tennis racket. When the psychiatrist questioned the parents on the wisdom of giving their son such a gift, they couldn't see that what they had done had been most insensitive. When he asked them whether it might have seemed to Bobby that they were telling him to go and walk in his brother's shoes – to go out and kill himself too, they responded: 'No, we didn't think about that. We're not educated people like you. We haven't

been to college and learned all kinds of fancy ways of thinking. We're just simple working people. We can't be expected to think of all these things.[9]' Actually they were perfectly intelligent people. The father was a precision tool maker
and the mother was a secretary for an insurance firm. They
just did not want to examine their actions. Scott Peck refers
to such folk as the 'People of the Lie'. 'We become evil,' he
says, 'by attempting to hide from ourselves.'[10]

AN OPEN-PLAN LIFE

Self-awareness is a very positive attitude and calls for a particular effort, which is to live an open-plan life. Last year we
stayed with some friends who had just moved into their
retirement home. The house gave the impression of being
big and airy, though in fact, it was quite small. The hallway
led into a large space that was the lounge, dining and
kitchen area – one naturally leading into the other. This
open-plan design gave a feeling of space and light. A person
who is self-aware is someone whose life is similarly designed
with no shut off areas, no locked doors, no skeletons in the
cupboard to jump out and surprise one. Everything is visible and available.

My experience of the rats in the cupboard is a good illustration of the way some people choose to live their lives. I
have told this story in an earlier book, but it's worth repeating. In 1959 David and I set sail for Chile with our luggage
and six-month-old baby daughter. On arrival we were sent
to live with a faithful, hard-working missionary couple in a
little frontier town called Chol Chol, an area known as
Araucania, where the Mapuche Indians lived. The dusty
roads, the murky bars and the cowboys riding horseback
into town made me think we had been transported into a
Hollywood Western. At any moment I expected to see John
Wayne coming out of one of the saloons – pistols drawn.
We quickly discovered that the house we shared with our
fellow missionaries had other occupants beside ourselves.

Whilst being shown around our new home we were taken into the kitchen. It was extremely basic, with no more than a table, some shelves, a sink and wood burning stove, which looked like (and probably was!) a piece of Victoriana! There was a closed door in one corner and I waited to be shown what was behind it. But our hostess ignored it. So I looked at it and asked her where it led. She replied that it was the storeroom, but it was never used, because it had rats. It was a year before our friends left to go on leave. During that year that storeroom door was never opened though the key hung on the wall. We lived with the inconvenience of having no larder in which to keep things, and we lived with the strange sounds of the vermin playing rat-games up and down the shelves. But our friends ignored it all, just as if it wasn't there.

When they left on leave we unlocked this door and spring cleaned the cupboard from top to bottom. We disinfected the shelves, blocked the holes and put the room to use once more. The cupboard could be entered. We now felt that every inch of the house was available to us – no locked doors, no nasty surprises – no rats in the cupboard![11]

Our hostess had been repulsed by the very thought of rats and had no inclination to face what was behind that door. Similarly, but with far greater consequences, Bobby's parents could not face asking themselves why they had given such a thoughtless present to their grieving son. Many people have 'rats' shut away in some cupboard of their lives and consciously or unconsciously they choose to keep it locked, and suffer the consequences. Why ever do people choose to live in such a manner?

LAZINESS AND CARELESSNESS
How many women avoid the bathroom scales because they do not want to know if they are over-weight? I am one of them! If I were to weigh myself I would know the truth and I am too reluctant to go on a specific diet or too lazy to take

more exercise than I already do. However, I have noticed that this in not just a female problem. Our doctor's surgery encourages us to have a check up with the nurse about once a year. I have to make encouraging noises to my husband for months before he eventually goes. I suspect he doesn't want to be told to take more exercise, lose weight, or watch his diet either. Such advice would upset his comfortable routine. Many people chose to turn a deaf ear to what they don't want to hear. In that way they can avoid having to deal with things they don't want to be bothered about. It takes discipline to change and that means effort, so we fail to notice what we don't want to notice. As R. D. Laing spells it out:

> The range of what we think and do
> is limited by what we fail to notice,
> And because we fail to notice
> *That* we fail to notice
> There is little we can do
> To change
> Until we notice
> How failing to notice
> Shapes our thoughts and deeds.

However, it may not be laziness – it may be just carelessness. We often move from one situation to another never stopping to take stock; never questioning ourselves; our motives, or the rightness of what we are doing. Then a situation arises which gives us an opportunity to review our lives and we realise how careless we have been. Such a chance was given to a young man called Mitch. After a gap of years he renewed contact with his old college professor, who was dying of an incurable illness. He visited him every Tuesday and on one occasion confessed to his teacher that he had traded lots of his dreams for a bigger pay cheque, adding: '*and I never realised I was doing it.*' On another visit he asked his old mentor about the important questions of life. The dying man replied: 'As I see it, they have to do with love, responsibility, spirituality and *awareness*' (italics mine).[12] Until those visits Mitch had been oblivious to the consequences of his choices. Only when he came face to face with the reality of death did he confront the truth about his life. It is significant that when Mitch asked about the important questions of life, one of the answers was 'awareness'.

Knowing the truth can be very challenging. It can also be very threatening.

FEAR

Flying back from holiday recently I was offered one of the dailies to read. Having no other reading matter with me I briefly scanned its pages. There was an article in it about Big Mo, from the soap opera, *EastEnders*. She had recently found a lump in her breast and had apparently delayed a month before seeing a doctor. The reason was fear. She was apprehensive about hearing the doctor's diagnosis.

Fear of knowing the truth is a big blockage to living an open-plan life. It's a dread of seeing things we would rather not see, and knowing things we would rather not know, because seeing and knowing would spell angst and pain. Parents may ignore the telltale signs that a child is being bullied, wanting to avoid the hassle of reporting it, or maybe even finding a new school. A church leader may ignore rumblings in his congregation, because he doesn't want to face his own wrong choices. I heard of one pastor in the USA whose church had shrunk from 900 members to 300 in a year, and he refused to admit that he might have been trying to take them in a wrong direction. A husband and father may take no notice of the growing unhappiness of his family because he doesn't want to change his lifestyle. A change could result in him never reaching the zenith of his profession. Such self-ish ambition often stems from the belief that only success will bring us satisfaction and bury a secret sense of worthlessness. Such unhealthy beliefs are often hidden but nevertheless hold sway over our behaviour.

HIDDEN BELIEFS

Oprah Winfrey calls these hidden attitudes 'shadow beliefs'. These may be the 'rats in the cupboard' we fear to examine too closely. When we visited our friends with the open-plan house they knew we would see them exactly as they were. There was nowhere to hide in their almost partition-less home. Any clutter, dust, or damage was there for all to see. A belief that people will not like us if they really see us warts and all, can be a real blockage to living genuinely open lives. When we live with self-doubt, self-hatred, and low self-esteem we not only live carefully with others but also with ourselves. The last thing we want is for someone else to recognise just how worthless we think we are. Nor do we want to examine ourselves too closely, afraid of having our worst fears confirmed. A very able lady once confessed that what she most feared was intimacy. She had no close friends because she kept everyone at arm's length and consequently was always lonely. Those who knew her viewed her as a highly capable and efficient woman. This super-competent front was her protection. People were a little awed and nervous around her, so they kept their distance. It was in a moment of extreme loneliness that she confessed to being afraid that if people really knew her they would not like her.

Our beliefs are not just accidents of nature. They are also the products of experience. The mind is at work all the time in every situation, consciously or unconsciously. We are making mental notes, drawing conclusions, recalling events, solving problems and anticipating our next move. Take for example a man hurrying to an appointment when he sees an acquaintance coming towards him. He assesses the situation and in an instant has planned how to make a quick getaway without appearing rude.

Most of the time we are relatively conscious of our

thought processes and we know why we have taken such and such an action. However, sometimes these actions seem quite spontaneous. We could not tell what we were thinking at the time. All we know is that we reacted in that way because it felt right, and not because of any rationalisation. Blaise Pascal in his *Pensées* wrote: 'The heart has its reasons that reason knows nothing of.' But behaviour is never senseless, though it may seem to be at first sight. Our thinking drives our behaviour, even though the thoughts may only be lurking in the shadows of our mind. The decision to live an open-plan life allows these beliefs to come to the surface and be brought out into the open. For example a child who loses her mother at the age of three, may only dimly remember it, but the experience of loss was so painful that somewhere in her unconscious mind she has decided to protect herself from anything similar ever happening to her again. Her inner reasoning is that people you love and need, leave you. Therefore it is safer not to depend upon, trust or love anyone too much ever again. The belief is buried in the unconscious but it nevertheless motivates her self-protective behaviour. She automatically switches off emotionally to anyone trying to get close, and cannot explain why she does it. Her behaviour will remain a mystery unless she decides to live an open-plan life and allow the painful memories of the past to come to the surface.

Fear of pain, challenge, change, and loss are major reasons for avoiding self-awareness. Yet another is an innate desire to become a person of significance.

AMBITION

When our identity is mistakenly attached to achievement, and our significance to greater and greater exploits we can become very driven people. Absalom was such a man. Although, his father, King David was still alive, Absalom wanted to be king in his father's place. His ambition even drove him to conspire against his father. He would get up early every morning and drive in his chariot and horses to the city gate. There he would greet, in a most friendly way, the people coming to the city to see his father. He would ask them what business they had and advise them sympathetically saying, 'Look, your claims are valid and proper, but there is no representative of the king to hear you.' And would add, 'If only I were appointed judge in the land! Then everyone who has a complaint or case could come to me and I would see that he receives justice!' In this way 'he stole the hearts of the men of Israel'. Absalom's ambition not only drove a wedge between himself and his father, but also between the people loyal to David and those being beguiled by his schemes.[13]

In recent years we have seen similar characters who have hit the headlines and will go down in the history books as people of raw, unscrupulous ambition. They were not men and women of truth because the truth would have blocked their rise to fame. In fact it was dishonesty and the distortion of truth which served their ambition most effectively. These people have lived with the belief that the end justified the means. They saw nothing wrong with wanting to get to the top. Therefore how they got there was immaterial. To look too closely at what they were doing would be to face the shameful truth, that they were really a nobody who imagined they could only become somebody by cheating and lying to everybody.

One such person was Robert Maxwell – the publishing magnate. He had started his life as an insignificant immigrant but by climbing over people and cheating, he became a famous, rich and prestigious businessman. Eventually his unscrupulous behaviour caught up with him and he died suddenly, amid rumours of suicide, leaving his sons to clear up the mess he had left behind. More recently there has been the lengthy trial of Lord Jeffrey Archer which ended in a four-year prison sentence for perjury and attempts to pervert the course of justice. According to the media it was his ambition to become the first mayor of London that precipitated his downfall. He began life as the son of a convicted con-man. Early in his life he began, like his father, to twist the truth to suit himself. He was accepted at Oxford University on the basis of a lie. Since then he has been hitting the headlines at intervals for one débâcle after another. In a television interview he confessed to being a good storyteller! Apparently his love of fiction didn't remain within the pages of his novels, but formed his natural thought patterns. A man who is unable to reach the top except by scheming and lying could not afford to examine his life too closely. The truth would be too devastating.

Twisting the truth for the sake of ambition isn't reserved just for men like Jeffery Archer. It could be easily done by any of us, though perhaps in less dramatic ways. The temptation to embellish a story a little to our advantage in order to look good in someone else's eyes is a common one. The desire to look more intelligent, and more important than we really are, is not unusual at all. Especially in a world where our value is so often measured by achievement, position and material gain. In such a society too many will consider it 'normal' to stretch the truth a little. In this way our conscience is gradually eroded and self-examination is avoided.

SOCIETY

Another factor in our slippery slide down the slope of lost integrity is that society and its institutions do not present us with a good model. It is normal for our leaders and bosses to use spin, hype and half-truths. Often we keep silent and go along with it rather than stand out as different. A young man we knew lost his job because he was not prepared to countenance the deception used by his firm. He could not lie and they would not continue to employ a man who refused to twist the truth *just a little*. The two just did not fit together. That is the society we live in. However, this is not an excuse for loosing our grip on truth, but it is one of the reasons that we give for doing it. We may have become compromised by the prevailing attitude to truth, but God has not changed his attitude towards it.

I can still blush with shame as I remember an incident that happened when we first moved to Chorleywood. I think God took advantage of a situation to teach me how highly he values the truth. Whether or not that was so, the fact is I certainly learned a hard and painful lesson. It was a Tuesday, our day off, and we had stayed in bed rather later than usual. It must have been about 9.30 am and we were still in bed, when the door bell rang. I hurriedly pulled on my jeans and ran down to the front door. On the doorstep was an elderly man whom I had seen vaguely in the distance on one or two occasions – a slightly peripheral member of the church, who had come to hand something in to David. He obviously noticed my rather dishevelled look and said he hoped he had not got me out of bed. In a desperate attempt to protect my image I instinctively responded in the negative. The moment that lie was uttered I felt guilty. But I consoled myself. 'After all it was just a little white lie, which would hurt no one.'

I buried the feelings and forgot the incident. But God did not! About a year later when I was attending an early morning prayer meeting the memory of that little 'white lie' came back, and with it the awful thought that God wanted me to confess my sin to the man to whom I had lied. 'No, God, you can't be serious.' I argued. But the thought would not go away. Finally I made a bargain with God. 'If this is you Lord, then you must set it up for me. Let the man come to the door this morning.' And to make it even more difficult, I added, 'And it has to be before 11 am.' Now I had not seen this man since the incident at the front door or if I had I had avoided him. I was 99.5% sure I would not see him that morning. I felt relaxed and safe. But I had not reckoned on God's desire and determination for me to become a person of truth.

At five minutes to eleven, just as I was congratulating myself on the fact that it must have been my imagination and not God speaking to me at all, the doorbell rang. I could not believe my eyes. There stood that very man! After all this time he had turned up again. Apparently he was an electrician and unbeknown to me David had asked him some weeks back if he would come and look at some electrical problem in the kitchen. I showed him in and left him talking to David while I disappeared upstairs where I had yet another argument with God. 'How can I do this?' I argued. 'He won't understand. He might not even be a Christian and this will make Christianity look stupid. And anyway I can't possibly say anything with David there. If you really want me to do this then you will have to remove David.'

I returned to the kitchen, hoping that all God had wanted was my willingness. But to my horror as I re-entered the kitchen David got up to go, asking me to give the man a cup of tea while he ran over to the office for a few minutes. I wished the floor would open and swallow me up. 'Why had I ever tried to protect my stupid image?' Eventually I gathered my courage and blurted out my confession. The poor man looked at me as if I needed my brains inspected, shook his head in a bemused sort of way and got on with his work. I don't expect he even remembers the conversation, but I will never forget it.[14]

Laziness, carelessness, fear, loss of reputation, hidden beliefs, ambition and social pressures are all reasons why we might ignore God's desire for 'truth in the inner parts.'[15] But we disregard it at our peril. Such neglect imposes a threat to our character, our relationships and our Christian witness. However, trying to live an open-plan life can be demanding. It makes one vulnerable to others who might feel free to criticise or challenge one now and again. It involves a willingness to hold one's life up to the scrutiny of Scripture, and the readiness to submit oneself to regular self-examination. Scott Peck stresses that a life totally dedicated to truth means that first of all it is a life of continuous and stringent self-examination.[16] For some this may appear too daunting; too time consuming; too out of character, or too introspective. But as I have already said it's not to do with self-absorption, but to do with the manner in which we live our lives. Once the decision has been made to live a life dedicated to truth, all that remains is to unlock the doors, knock a few walls down and re-arrange the furniture. Once the alterations have been made, then it is a case of keeping an open heart and mind, and using every opportunity to change the things we see wrong.

However, simply agreeing that self-awareness is needful, is not enough of a motive for most of us. A more serious reason is required before we will subject ourselves to such discipline.

Chapter Three

KNOW GOD,
KNOW YOURSELF

*'Men and women cannot know themselves until they
know the reality of the God who made them.'*[1]

Becoming a healthily self-conscious person is a totally biblical concept. In fact without an awareness of our sinfulness
we would never seek cleansing and forgiveness. St John
encourages us to walk in the light as God is in the light.
Nothing can be hidden when the light is shining.
Everything is open to scrutiny. Forgiveness and fellowship
are made possible when we are open with ourselves, with
God and with one another.[2] In fact 'awakenings' are so
named because at such times people wake up to the reality
of their state before God. They realise their true condition –
the scales are removed from their eyes. They become conscious of their sin and their need of God's forgiveness. A
spiritual 'awakening' makes self-knowledge easier.
Therefore when the awakening power that comes with a
revival is not so obviously at work then it's even more
important that we form the wholesome discipline of self-
examination.

Timothy had responsibility for the church in Ephesus,
which was the biggest church in the most important city of
Asia Minor. With such a visible position Paul knew that
Timothy must take care how he lived his life. Timothy was

still a young man. Though Paul spoke of him to the Philippians with great affection, and underlined his traits of loyalty and sensitivity,[3] he also knew that Timothy struggled with timidity and lustful thoughts,[4] tendencies that could prove dangerous to his ministry. Hidden and unrecognised weaknesses can easily trip us up and may prove especially damaging to a person in leadership. I heard recently of two young leaders who decided to make themselves accountable to one another. They gave each other permission to view the other's computer at any time and to inspect what internet sites they had each been surfing. Knowing the easy access to pornographic sites and the trap they become, especially to someone in Christian ministry, they had decided it wise to build in a safety net.

Understanding the danger of hidden weakness, and the corresponding strength of temptation, Paul gave Timothy some wise advice. 'Watch your life and doctrine closely. Persevere in them, because if you do, you will save both yourself and your hearers.'[5] Literally Paul was advising Timothy to pay attention to himself and his doctrine, those two things, self-awareness and knowing the character and requirements of God, would be the best protection against the entrapment of sin. Such awareness would be a safety net, not just for Timothy, but also for those to whom he was seeking to minister.

It is significant that Paul linked self-awareness with knowing doctrine. Doctrine has to be the starting point. It is the revelation of God's truth. It not only gives us the motive for self-examination but it is also the plumbline by which we should measure our lives.

THE REASON FOR SELF-EXAMINATION
In the beginning we find God making man and woman in his image, and placing them in a wonderful garden from which they were to rule over his creation. God would come and walk with them in the cool of the day and have fellow-

ship with them. Being made in God's image gave them the ability to relate intimately with him. Although God told them clearly what they could and could not do, he also gave them the power to make choices. If they did make the wrong decision and disobey him, he knew that their spirits would surely die and their intimacy with him would fade. As we know Adam and Eve gave in to Satan's temptation and as a result they lost their relationship with God, and their image of him was marred. It was a monumental tragedy for mankind, but not the end of the story.

God still wanted a people for himself. And he started afresh with Abram when he called him out of his country and promised him a land. He made a covenant with Abram telling him: 'I will make you into a great nation and I will bless you; I will make your name great, and you will be a blessing. I will bless those who bless you, and whoever curses you I will curse; and all peoples on earth will be blessed through you.'[6] Later this covenant is reiterated with a proper ritual and Abram is promised a son and offspring that would equal the stars in the sky in number. 'Abram believed the Lord, and he credited it to him as righteousness.'[7] But his descendants failed to go on trusting God. They were blessed by God but never became the blessing to the world that God had intended.

God has not changed his mind. It is still his plan to have a people for himself; a people who bear his image; a people whom he can bless and who will be a blessing to the nations around them. This is God's amazing plan – his story. But we all have our own stories. Because of our brokenness we are left with many unmet needs within us that cry out to be satisfied. Most of us start the Christian life with great enthusiasm. We want God's agenda for our lives. However, self-deception is endemic. The bias towards independence and the magnetic draw of getting our needs met, gradually and insidiously distracts us from God's plans and into our own. Often we don't even realise what we are doing. We start off wanting God's will and we end up doing our own thing. The unmet needs for love, and for significance cry out for our attention. Being so often unaware of what we do, we begin to meet those needs in ways that are unhelpful and far short of God's purposes for us. Only as we open our eyes and take a good look at ourselves and where we are in God's story, do we become aware of how far off we have strayed. Then we are so relieved to find that the cross is still the way back into the centre of God's will and that this is truly the only place where our needs can be fully met. Because of this temptation to be knocked off course into our own little agendas we need to be constantly vigilant and open to self-examination.

Understanding God's purposes becomes an excellent spur for becoming more self-aware. We may get side-tracked but nothing can knock God off track. He still wants a people for himself. And to get his plan back on the road, God sent Jesus, to mend both the broken relationship and the marred image. In one sense because we are 'in Christ' we are already perfect – the image has been restored. But in another sense we are still in the process of being trans-formed. We are still being changed and so long as we remain on earth that work will continue – but only with our co-operation. God would rarely violate our own free will. We have to want to change and work with God in becoming like him. I think this is what Paul meant when he wrote that we must continue to work out our salvation, or wholeness, with fear and trembling. For it is God who works in us according to his good purpose.[8] We have to work out what God is working in us. The goal of becoming like God is worth striving for. That was God's plan for us from the beginning. 'For those God foreknew he also *predestined* to be conformed to the likeness of his Son, that he might be the firstborn among many brothers'[9] (italics mine).

Knowing this gives us a good reason for examining our lives. Are we becoming like Jesus? Are we reflecting God's image? Are we co-operating with God in his plan to bless us and change us that we might become a blessing? Or are we off at some tangent of our own making – meeting our own needs?

GOD'S CHARACTER IS THE PLUMBLINE

If we are to reflect God's image then we must know the character of God. Obviously we could fill books about God and find we haven't even begun. But there is an aspect of the character of God that is paramount. It stands out above all other characteristics, and that is his holiness. It is an essential element of God's nature that is required of his people.

God is Holy!

'Who among the gods is like you, O Lord? Who is like you – majestic in holiness, awesome in glory, working wonders?'[10] So sang Moses and Miriam after they had crossed the Red Sea. God clearly expects his people to reflect this special quality. God told Moses to tell the people to 'Consecrate yourselves and be holy, because I am the Lord your God. Keep my decrees and follow them. I am the Lord, who makes you holy.'[11] This injunction is carried forward into the New Testament when Peter reminds the disciples of Christ to 'be holy in all you do; for it is written: "Be holy, because I am holy."'[12] Jesus certainly expected that the lives of his disciples would reflect the holiness of God. In the Sermon on the Mount Jesus challenges his disciples to be different from the pagans, and to 'be perfect . . . as your heavenly Father is perfect.'[13]

In order to reflect God's holiness we have to walk in the light, noticing the imperfections, ready to straighten out any flaws. Holiness is the overarching characteristic of God that we should be striving to emulate, but within that comes another attribute that we should pursue.

God is a God of Truth

Both King David and the prophet Isaiah spoke of God as 'the God of truth'[14] – a God who desires that his people have truth in the inner parts.[15] To be holy as God is holy demands that we become seekers after truth. We are called to live lives that demonstrate this facet of God's character. It has always been important but now more so than ever. We can no longer rest in the knowledge that the truth is to be trusted and believed. As Os Guinness writes, 'The dawn of the third millennium finds the western world in a quandary over one of its most vital foundations – truth. Caught between a tarnished modernism and a dangerous post-modernism, between a view of truth (part arrogant and part naïve) that is no longer credible and a view of "truth" (part sceptical and part gullible) that every day grows less desirable, the West is at odds with itself, its past and its future.'[16]

Jesus told his disciples to hold to his teaching. 'If you hold to my teaching, you are really my disciples. Then you will know the truth, and the truth will set you free.'[17] Paul advises Timothy to know his doctrine. Biblical doctrine is truth and as we live by it, making it the plumbline for our lives we will begin to experience an amazing freedom from guilt and a bad conscience. The light of Scripture will shine on our lives and nothing will be left lurking in the darkness, unconfessed and unforgiven – no skeletons in the cupboard. In fact one of the tasks of the Holy Spirit, who is called the Spirit of truth, is to lead us into all truth.[18]

GOD IS A GOD OF LOVE

John the disciple whom Jesus loved wrote his first letter almost exclusively about love. 'God is love', he announced.[19] Therefore like him we must love one another. Loving entails walking in the light and speaking the truth in love to one another. About twenty years ago I was sharing an umbrella with a friend. It was a typically wet evening in London and we were on our way to a conference. The friend was a person I had only recently come to know and we were not particularly close. In fact I was not looking for a close relationship. I was busy with a family and church concerns and felt very fulfilled and satisfied with that. As we walked along my friend commented that I was rather difficult to get to know. I was a little surprised at her frankness and quickly came to my own defence. 'Well, actually I don't particularly need other people – in fact I am a bit of a loner,' I responded. 'Really,' she replied, 'well that's not very biblical.' I was stopped in my tracks. 'What do you mean?' I demanded. 'Well, perhaps you should go home and read John chapter seventeen,' she responded quietly. I was annoyed and decided that nothing would induce me to read it. But by the time I arrived home I had simmered down and my curiosity got the better of me. I read through the whole of John 17. At first I couldn't see why she had highlighted that particular passage, until I came to the bit where Jesus prayed for his disciples and said, 'Holy Father, protect them by the power of your name – the name you gave me – so that they may be one as we are one.'[20]

Suddenly I saw the inconsistency of my life in the mirror of God's word. Jesus wanted his disciples to enjoy the same oneness as he and his Father enjoyed. The closeness and intimacy was so glorious that I had often commented on it in talks. In fact books have been written on just that aspect of Jesus' life. And Jesus' longed that his followers (which I professed to be!) would have that same oneness. With the recognition came repentance. I knew that a change had to take place. Now between recognising that particular flaw and changing, what was for me a habitual stance, time was needed. It took effort and courage to bridge the gulf between where I was and where I wanted to be. Change usually happens slowly and only in so far as one is prepared to take risks with new behaviour. But eventually I, and even my new friend, could see the difference!

However, knowing that God is a God of love doesn't

only give us an example to follow, but also reassures – God loves us. He is for us not against us. He loved us enough to give his own Son to die for us. He is 100% committed to us, and longs for us to bear the family likeness. Just as there is joy in a family when one of the children shows the same good traits as his father, or the same grace as the mother, so God rejoices when he sees his characteristics developing in us.

Just the other day we had an illustration of this in the family. One of our daughters was moving. The house they were moving into needed some building work and repainting. It was hard to oversee this work from a distance and they had to rely on the builders reading the instructions they left for them. But along the way some mistakes were made. Just before they moved they discovered that the painters had muddled which room was for which boy and it was too late to re-paint, so it meant that two of the boys had to change bedrooms. The boys already knew which rooms they were to have and had for weeks been telling all their friends how 'cool' their particular room was. Now the news had to be broken. Two of them would have to swap. One was too young to be that interested but the other was definitely interested! My daughter hesitated before telling him not wanting to disappoint him. But he takes after his paternal Grandmother, who is one of the most positive women ever born. When Sebastian heard the news he said: 'Cool, it's bigger!' And then went on to talk about something else on his mind. Once again, as often before, Seb had revealed that positive family trait.

Changing to become like God and portraying his character should be as joyful. It should not be a legal headache, something that will weigh heavily upon us as a duty, but it should be a labour of love – a delight. Something which can be worked at together with our Heavenly Father who loves us more than we can ever know. It is easy to lose the impact, and therefore the benefit of this fact – that God loves us. The major blockage to knowing it is unbelief. Not unbelief that God is a God of love and that he loves the world, but unbelief that he loves me! 'Oh, yes,' we say to ourselves, 'I believe God loves everyone. But some people he favours and those are the ones that he loves in an individual and special way. He loved Paul and Timothy. He loves the people who sit on platforms, or who have great gifts, but I am not important enough for God to have even noticed me!' So we accept that God loves the world. But not that he knows, cares for and is concerned about every individual. Many people secretly have this attitude and as a result never have within them the urgency and longing to please their Heavenly Father and to become like him. For this reason it is vital that we take time to search the Scriptures until we know the truth about God, and his character. Only then can we really start knowing ourselves.

First then God's plan to have a people of his own who are like him gives us the reason for examining ourselves. Secondly God's character and teaching become the plumbline against which we examine our lives. Then all that is left is to do the hard work of self-examination.

KNOW YOURSELF

The major problem we face when trying to know ourselves is self-deception. We are very clever at deceiving ourselves rather than face any sort of discomfort. 'We do not deal in facts,' said Mark Twain, 'when we are contemplating ourselves.' So what are the steps necessary to begin the journey into self-awareness?

Acknowledgement

First of all we each have to come to the decisive point in our lives when we acknowledge to ourselves, and to God, that change and transformation is part of his plan for our lives. It is not enough to think that change would be a good idea, nor is it enough to make an intellectual assent to it as an idea. It has to be a personal, heartfelt agreement that God wants me to be like him so that we can relate to him in intimacy, be blessed by him personally, and as a result become the blessing he has always intended his children should be to the world around.

Recognition

The next step to self-knowledge is the realisation that we are all capable of deceiving ourselves. 'There is an almost gravitational pull toward putting out of mind unpleasant facts. We tune out, we turn away, we avoid. Finally we forget, and forget we have forgotten.'[21] But by ignoring the 'rats in the cupboard' and pretending that everything in our lives is fine, we will never experience the changes necessary if our lives are to have any integrity at all. 'You cannot change what you do not acknowledge. And what you do not acknowledge is going to get worse until you do.'[22] We all have a tendency to repetitive behaviour, even when the outcome is continuously negative. Becoming aware of the pattern and the motivation behind our actions is the only protection we have. Nor is it just recognition that something in our lives is wrong and needs changing; it is also owning the responsibility for what is wrong. We have to recognise that we choose our behaviour for the results it produces.

When we constantly repeat behaviour that gives the same results every time, it stands to reason that the results must be achieving something. In other words there is a payoff of some sort. If this were not so we would have stopped. It is important that we recognise this reality. Even when our behaviour is apparently producing negative results this principle is still operative. At first it may be difficult to see the pay-off. For example why would a person continue to overeat when such a habit will only damage health? Well the long term pay-off is negative, but what about the short-term satisfaction? What need is being met by the eating? Is it just hunger and lack of discipline or is it to do with loneliness, compensation for dissatisfaction in life, or unhappiness, which food momentarily appeases?

What about the woman who constantly nags her husband because he is so passive, lacking in ambition and uncommunicative. The result of her nagging is that he withdraws even more and achieves less than ever. Why would she continue such unrewarding behaviour? There must be a pay-off somewhere! Perhaps the feeling of being top-dog gives her a sense of importance. Perhaps she gets pleasure out of comparing herself to him, and seeing him as weak and herself as strong.

The only way we will change such negative behaviour is when we admit to the real motivation behind it. "You cannot eliminate your negative behaviour without understanding why you do it to begin with. Only then will you know what buttons to push to get the desired change in your own behaviour or that of others."[23] Only honest and careful self-examination will uncover the hidden agendas we all carry. Without it we will continue to repeat self-defeating behaviour 'ad infinitum'.

Recognising and admitting our inclination, and our ability to hide from any unpleasant truth about ourselves is an important step towards eventual self-awareness. However, it is one thing to recognise this tendency in ourselves, it is another to decide to face the truth whatever the cost.

Decision

In so many cases we run away the moment we come close to truly seeing ourselves. Scott Peck describes an incident which happened in his first year of psychiatric training. A patient recounted a dream he had had which seemed, in Scott Peck's eyes, to indicate some anxiety over his sexual orientation. Wanting to appear a knowledgeable therapist Scott Peck confronted his client and told him, much too bluntly, that his dream obviously showed some concerns with homosexuality. As a result the man grew visibly anxious and did not keep his next three appointments. Though he did eventually come back into therapy he never would face his anxiety.[24]

'Honesty means the truth; the whole truth, the unvarnished; ugly truth. It takes courage and commitment to be brutally, genuinely honest with yourself.'[25] We have to make a deal with ourselves that we will take the blindfold off our eyes, and we will bravely face the facts about ourselves. We must face the pain, even the shame of self-discovery. But in making such a decision we must continuously remind ourselves that God is on our side. He loves us. He is committed to us. And if we stay with his agenda, he will work everything out for our good in the end.[26]

I was recently speaking on the subject of knowing ourselves and on the wall behind the stage where I was standing was a large picture of an outstretched hand and next to that a huge cross. I encouraged my listeners to make the hand and the cross the back-drop to all I was saying. I wanted them to be reminded of God's love and of the safety of making a trusting response. Within that secure relationship, they could face every challenge.

Request

David bravely requested God to examine him and to know him.[27] We must move from decision to action. But soul searching should never be done in isolation. The Holy Spirit has been sent especially to lead us into truth. At the same time he is there to comfort us and strengthen us. If we truly desire to know the truth he will take us by the hand and gently lead us to a place of acceptance. But at the same time he will be there to protect us from our fears, to deal with our shame and to strengthen our wills to change.

Again and again I have seen him uncover the secrets that people have been hiding from themselves for years. One woman hated being left alone in a house, but couldn't fathom why. With some friends she asked the Holy Spirit to uncover the truth she was unconsciously afraid to face. At first her mind just skated around her fear. Then she began to have a picture of the gloomy dinning room in her childhood home, and with that memory came the feeling that there was someone hiding there. But she couldn't bring herself to look and see who it was. One of her friends made the strange suggestion that she should ask God to show her the shoes of whoever was in the room. Following that request she looked and saw a pair of brown brogues and in that instance knew it was a lodger who had once tried to touch her inappropriately. Apparently one of her friends had asked God to reveal who had been in the room and had immediately had a picture of a pair of brown brogues, and felt sure her frightened friend would recognise them. The security of knowing the Holy Spirit is in control is incredibly reassuring. It gives us the courage, as nothing else does, to open up to the truth.

However, a decision to take action and prayer for the Holy Spirit to accompany us on our quest for truth, comes only after we have first recognised and then relinquished the strategies we have used to protect ourselves from facing it.

Chapter Four

AVOIDING THE TRUTH

'As human beings we are by nature truth-seekers; as fallen human beings we are also by nature truth twisters.'[1]

Twisting the truth and avoiding the truth is as old as history itself. Early in the story of God's people Jacob, the son of Isaac, became known for his deceiving ways. But he gets his 'come-uppance' when he is tricked into marrying Leah instead of his true love, Rachel. His father-in-law, Laban, turns out to be as big a deceiver as himself. The world has moved on since then, but we haven't grown out of those artful wiles. Jacob used trickery to obtain two things he greatly coveted – his birthright and his father's blessing. Laban deceived Jacob by marrying him to Leah, because he didn't want to be shamed by breaking with culture and marrying his younger daughter off before his older. We may have grown a little more subtle and clever in the way we manipulate the truth, but the reasons we do it are the same. It benefits us in some way.

We have invented a myriad of ways to deceive ourselves. The following list is by no means comprehensive, but as we read it let's be prepared to stop at intervals and allow the light of the Holy Spirit to scrutinise our hearts. Let's stop and ask ourselves the difficult questions, 'Have I avoided the truth? What are the reasons? And if I have how am I doing it?' It takes courage to face up to such questions because it is easier to continue as we are than to live a life of dedication to the truth. But it is only the courage to seek the truth, and to speak it, that can save us from the narcotic of self-deception.[2]

Some of the methods we use to dupe ourselves and others are so mild they would come into the category of harmless white lies. But lies nevertheless! At times they are unconscious, and at other times deliberately conscious strategies. However, understanding and change go hand in hand. If we are to become more like Jesus we have to understand why we have this propensity for avoiding the truth, as well as the personalised method we have invented to do it. Some of the most compelling reasons are our desire for comfort, security, and peace; other reasons are to do with saving face, looking good, and a strange need we have occasionally to play with fire and not be found out.

PEACE AT ALL COSTS

Few people like being disturbed. Most of us will seek a peaceful route through our problems if we can. However, there are times when we can be too attached to our peace of mind. Rather than face up to painful issues we ignore them.

As a child one of my most exciting outings was to attend a 'Point to Point' race meeting. However, it always bothered me to see one or two of the horses wearing blinkers. It looked so uncomfortable and dangerous for them to be limited in what they could see. My brother, who was a jockey, would explain to me that it was necessary to blinker a horse if he had the tendency to shy away from anything he saw moving out of the corner of his eye. The only answer to this problem was to cause the horse to see with tunnel vision. His view might be restricted but at least he ran the race without becoming distracted or frightened.

Tunnel vision or blind spots

We may unconsciously choose to limit our view when we do not want our peace disturbed by difficult or painful circumstances. Another name for tunnel vision is 'selective inattention', or 'selective attention'. We decide what to attend to and what to leave beyond the periphery of our awareness. This strategy edits from experience those elements that might be unsettling were one to notice them.[3] Even though the strategy appears involuntary, nevertheless, at some level, we have made a choice to keep the uncomfortable information outside our view. In fact if we were to stop and ask ourselves why we were feeling slightly anxious, we could quite easily find the reason.

Similarly blind spots are aspects of life we choose not to notice. They are there in front of our eyes but we act as if they were not there. It can be a dangerous ploy if it prevents us from taking necessary action. Occasionally the delay between refusing to notice and eventually being forced to see the truth can be disastrous. A woman I once knew was a shopaholic. Every day she would spend money on things she didn't need, and the bills mounted up. She was massively in debt but continued as if she had all the money in the world, and ignored the bills as if they didn't exist. It was a very bad day when her husband eventually found out, and she was brought face to face with her addiction.

Terminal illness is one of the most difficult experiences to deal with in the church family, especially for a church that believes in healing. We heard of one situation where a wife had developed cancer and her husband was determined that she would be healed. The church prayed faithfully for her, but despite their prayers she began to go downhill and was obviously dying. However, the husband could not accept her condition and refused to see the signs of deterioration. When she did eventually die he and the children were completely unprepared. There had been no preparation for her death and no proper goodbyes were said. No one wants to have their hopes and dreams shattered, or their peace disrupted, but the consequences of taking the route of blanking out disturbing data can be worse.

A mother may ignore the fact that her beautiful teenage daughter is missing her meals and becoming thinner by the day. She doesn't want to contemplate the thought that she might be suffering from anorexia or bulimia. Every now and again she suffers slight anxiety but she pushes it away refusing to allow the worry to surface into full awareness, because she cannot bear to face the painful knowledge that ahead could lie a huge problem that could destroy her daughter and their family life. But the delay could mean the difference between healing and a life threatening illness.

A father may ignore his wife's plea for him to spend more time with their teenage son. He may refuse to notice the boy's growing alienation from the family. Even though the boy is sullen and rude, still the father excuses the behaviour as being 'just his age'. His wife begs him to change his attitude; take him out; to talk to him and find out what is happening. Still the man insists that all is well and that he sees nothing unusual. In fact he can't face the fact that he has been neglecting his young family all their lives, and doesn't know how to make it up to them. He may be basically a lazy man who enjoys his golf on Saturdays, and can't energise himself enough to change his ways. He is eventually forced into noticing when his son takes an overdose and is rushed into hospital.

Failing to notice uncomfortable facts may endanger other people's lives and may on occasions endanger even our own. Larry Hagman who became famous for playing J. R. Ewing in the soap opera *Dallas*, was an alcoholic. He drank heavily most of his life but always made light of it. 'No,' he said, 'drinking was never a problem – until I needed a new liver.'[4] He refused to see that alcohol was killing him until it was almost too late. Larry is fortunate to be alive, not because he recognised what he was doing and stopped drinking in time, but because he received an organ transplant, and now functions on the liver of a 35-year-old.

Without noticing we can easily be distracted by our

desire to have an easy life, to feel secure, or to feel important. We start the Christian life well, determined to put
God's will first, before all else. But the enemy knows our
places of weakness, and our basic needs will always cry out
to be met. It is tempting to take short cuts to procure that
which our soul longs for. It is then that a mother can place
her own desire for peace before the health of her daughter,
and a man can place his need for comfort before responsibility for his family.

Such strategy is one of the easiest ways of avoiding
uncomfortable truths. Most of us have employed it at one
time or another. If a certain behaviour rewards us by making us feel good, or by giving us an adrenaline rush, we may
choose not to listen to our consciences. It is this mechanism
which keeps us from making a hasty exit in a dangerous situation. A married man may not immediately change his secretary when he first feels attracted to her; instead he plays with
fire, and may eventually cheat on his wife, ruining his marriage, and hurting his children as a result. A young leader
may be continually warned about his flirtatiousness with the
girls in the youth club, but he repeatedly denies that he is
doing anything wrong. In fact he uses the age-old tactic of
deflection whenever the subject is raised. He cleverly diverts
attention on to another topic of conversation. Tunnel vision
can keep people in a church where the leader has become
manipulative and unable to take any sort of criticism, or
questioning. They turn a blind eye to the signs that their
beloved church is becoming more and more like a cult,
rather than face the pain of upsetting or leaving their
friends, and giving up all they have invested in the way of
time, money and energy.

The reason for tunnel vision is basically a selfish one.
Therefore it derails us from God's will and leads us off at a
tangent and into our own agendas.

Displacement

Another strategy our devious minds have invented to keep us from being disturbed is displacement. This is a mechanism employed by those who do not want to acknowledge or own their real fear, so they displace it on to something else-something that usually has some slight resemblance to what they actually fear.

Scott Peck tells the story of a young teenage girl called Billie who entered therapy with a colleague of his. She was sixteen and very bright but was underachieving at school. After six months her grades improved and so her mother said the problem was solved. However, Billie liked her therapist and decided to continue with him. Her mother refused to pay for it but Billie found the money herself and stayed in therapy for another seven years. She had no particular symptoms or reasons for continuing, except that she wanted to do better at school.

The only other thing that could possibly be called a symptom was her fear of spiders. She suffered from arachnophobia. Apparently Billie's father was a quiet, undemonstrative man for whom she had little time, but her mother was her closest friend. They told each other everything. After Billie left college her therapist encouraged her to get an apartment of her own. It was then that Billie faced her terror of being alone. She would frequently drive back to her mother's house and stay the night. But after a while Billie decided that at least one night a week she would stay at her own place. She chose Wednesday evenings. Every Wednesday, just as Billie prepared to leave her mother's house for her apartment, her mother would bring up some very provocative topic for discussion, and so she would stay on. For ten weeks she struggled to go to her own place, but her mother always found a way to prevent her.

After while Billie began to challenge her mother about what she was doing. Then her mother would cry and so once more Billie would stay. As her mother became more and more clinging Billie's fear of spiders became even worse. She had reached the stage when she wanted to be in her own apartment, but at the mention of leaving her mother would become hysterical. Describing one such episode to her therapist Billie suddenly commented, 'She was like a goddamn spider.' 'I've been waiting a long time for you to say that,' her therapist responded.

It had been too difficult for Billie to acknowledge her fear of her mother. What child wants to hate her mother? So she had displaced her fear onto spiders, who spin their webs and trap their prey. In the same way Billie had been caught in the trap of her mother's need.[5]

I remember meeting a person who suffered from agoraphobia. She found it very hard to leave the safety of her home and did so only with great difficulty. But her real fear was death. She had witnessed a frightening accident as a child and had gradually displaced her fear of sudden death on to open spaces. Scott Pecks tells of a man who would walk three blocks out of his way rather than walk past a funeral parlour and if a hearse drove by he would duck into a doorway or run into a department store rather than have to see the hearse. He insisted that he wasn't afraid of death, 'It's just those damn hearses and funeral parlours that bother me.'[6] Displacement usually occurs when the real cause of our anxiety is too traumatic to face, at least in our perception. It is most evidently seen in cases of phobias, but it can also occur in less obvious traits or ways.

We see displacement in children who have been the victims of parental cruelty and abuse. There is no way they can show how angry they are with their parents, so instead they vent it on animals or other children. Or adults who are having a miserable time at the office may come home and take their frustration out on the family. Another form of displacement occurs when we are unable to own our unacceptable or shameful feelings so we project them on to others. The anger or rejection I feel towards a friend is repressed, only to surface as his rejection of me. It becomes the other person's problem not mine. I once talked to a young man who told me how quick he was to recognise anyone with any homosexual leanings. He said he felt very disgusted by such people. But later he confessed to being anxious about his own sexual orientation.

Forgetting

This is another way of having peace, but at the cost of losing a bit of one's life. 'Repression has come to mean the defence wherein one forgets, then forgets one has forgotten.'[7] Rape or childhood incest is often buried in the unconscious rather than suffer the pain of remembering. Or it maybe frightening impulses that are quickly pushed out of mind. We can't accept the idea that we would want to kill our own mother, but then wonder why we become anxious when left alone with her. I once agreed to see a young boy who had suddenly developed obsessive thoughts that led to some rather bizarre behaviour, mostly to do with cleanliness. I asked him if he could remember when they had started. I was surprised when he said that they had begun one night when he was in the bath. 'Did something happen that night?' I asked him. 'I had a bad thought about my mother.' He replied. I asked him what it was. But he couldn't remember. He was just left with some peculiar fears.

Meg was a young girl who suffered from a strange phobia. She was terrified of men. She asked for help because she was becoming embarrassed and tired of her abnormal response to the close proximity of the opposite sex. Whenever a male came too close she would react as if she had an allergy. First she would find it hard to breathe, then she would start to hyperventilate and, if escape was impossible, she would pass out. When asked what she was afraid of she had no answer. She couldn't remember any traumatic event involving a man. Meg was a girl who had forgotten what had happened and then forgotten that she had forgotten. The trauma of her childhood abuse had been too painful to be allowed to remain in her conscious mind so she placed it outside of her awareness. But her unconscious had not forgotten – hence her strange reaction, that did not seem so bizarre when the facts came to light. Humans have an amazing capacity to play games with their minds in the service of self-preservation. Anxiety stands like a sentinel at the gateway to consciousness preventing uncomfortable facts from passing into awareness.

Children under great stress will try and disassociate from the pain and terror. One young woman said she would concentrate on the wallpaper in her bedroom while she was being violated. 'I would almost become a part of it,' she said. Many sexual abuse victims manage to repress the knowledge and forget the horror of what happened to them. The trouble is that rats in the cupboard smell. Flashbacks, dreams, mental health problems, physical illness tend to haunt such a person until they uncover the truth, face the pain, and eventually put the past to rest.

Having said this, let me add that one must always beware of the false memory syndrome. It is easy to add two and two and make five in the counselling room. Just because a person suffers the above symptoms does not mean that they have been sexually molested, and no counsellor should ever make such a suggestion. If the memories come back to a victim and s/he knows without a shadow of doubt that s/he was abused, then the counsellor is free to take it from there.

GETTING AWAY WITH IT!

It's hard to accept that a Christian man or woman would want to 'get away' with something that is blatantly wrong. But there is a tendency within all of us to think that that which no one else knows about, or that which we think would harm no one else, doesn't matter. So we use a common strategy – compartmentalising or partitioning.

Compartmentalising

This ploy is similar to tunnel vision except that it is more of a deliberate policy. When we compartmentalise we make a conscious choice to cordon off a part of life that may be unpleasant by putting it into a separate department so that we can go on living as if it wasn't there.[8] It is the opposite to living an open-plan life.

The Rev Jesse Jackson, the black civil rights leader, was recently found to have had an illegitimate child by one of his office staff. He may have been having the affair during the time that he was actually counselling Bill Clinton during the Monica Lewinsky trial. Certainly around that time Jackson had paid the woman £25,000 to be relocated and was paying maintenance of £2,000 a month and hoping, no doubt, that his indiscretion would not be discovered. Jesse Jackson had been married for thirty-eight years, had five children, and was a confessing Christian leader. Yet by an act of compartmentalising he was able to live a public life, preaching and counselling another man in a sordid sex scandal, and at the same time have an affair with a Miss Stanford.[9]

Bill Clinton was a past master at the art of partitioning. He most likely learned the strategy from his mother. She wrote in her autobiography, 'Whatever is in someone's past is past, and I don't need to know about it . . . When bad things do happen, I brainwash myself to put them out of my mind.'[10] It was Clinton's ability to cordon off unpleasant realities of life that led to the CNN's term 'the split-screen presidency' and to a leading journalist's damning description of the 'Jekyll and Hyde' personalities of the 'Sunday morning president' (or daylight Clinton) and 'Saturday night Bill' (or 'Clinton noir').[11]

It is easy for us to condemn such blatantly shameful behaviour, and ignore the fact that compartmentalising is almost as common as tunnel vision. It is similar to having an unruly teenager in the house. Most parents shut the door on the poster clad walls and the mess between! Some older people still keep the equivalent of an unruly teenager in their lives and rather than exercise some discipline they shut the door and let the mess amass. We so often live with the belief that what happens in private is our business and does not affect our public lives. So we watch pornography, violent movies, row with our spouse, shout at the children, become manipulative when things go wrong and privately live a selfish life – then we go to church on Sunday as if everything in our life was in perfect order.

Richard Dortch, the man who went to prison for fraud after the Tammy and Jimmy Bakkar débâcle in the USA, had the reputation as a man of integrity. But he began to close his eyes and refused to admit to the things he saw happening around him. He was mentally shutting doors and failing to examine the mess that was accumulating behind them. He said that he realised that his integrity was being slowly eroded, but felt powerless to flee from the slippery slope. Dortch had shielded Jimmy Bakker after the latter had had an affair with a woman and avoided telling the truth about the money used to pay her off. Later he argued with himself saying, 'I didn't have an affair with Jessie Hahn. I wasn't involved in any immoral activity. I haven't stolen any money. Here I am in the middle of what could explode into a national disgrace. How did I get myself into this mess?' And he wept and asked himself the questions. 'Was it ever right to stretch the truth? Is it ever judicious to tell a lie to protect someone else? Does the end justify the means?' This is what he had done and he paid a very high price for it.[12]

In his book, aptly entitled *Integrity, How I Lost It and My Journey Back*, he says that in the many years that he had served as a leader he had noticed that almost everyone who had fallen, both leader and laymen, did so because they believed an exception would be made in their case. They thought that they could pick and choose. They could sin . . . even if only occasionally . . . even for a good cause, and it would make no difference. They could have a public persona but no one would ever see the other side of their life.[13]

By compartmentalising we get away with practices that we want to keep from public view. Sometimes however, the activity is in the open and what we want to hide is the motive behind it. Then, in order to get away with it we rationalise.

Rationalisation

This strategy may be used by an individual or a group wanting to cover over something, which could make them look bad, with a 'cloak of reasonableness'.[14]

Governments, businesses, men, women and children may all employ this strategy at times. We make the excuse that what we are trying to persuade people to do, or to believe, is something that in the end, will be beneficial all round. In other words 'the end justifies the means'. Usually the bottom line is that it is for our personal benefit. It will make us feel better, or look good. We can be so persuasive that we can even believe our own story! A Government continually has to explain why it has granted money to one group and not to another. When people want to avoid giving the real reasons behind their decisions, they give the public 'spin' – another term for rationalising. A firm might fudge the facts about its product to make more sales. The board then agrees together that the fudging won't do anyone any harm, and in any case by making more profit they can employ more people and that can only be good for the economy generally. None of them openly admits that it will enhance their own personal income also!

It's a tactic used by men and women who do not have enough self-esteem to be honest about their true motives. Saul used it to cover up his jealousy and evil designs on David. Wanting to kill David because he felt so threatened by his popularity and anointing, Saul pursued him from place to place. When David took refuge in the town of

Keilah, Saul openly declared that God had delivered David
into his hands, which made his actions sound righteous.[15]
In fact his vindictive behaviour was because of his jealousy
and had nothing to do with the will of God. God was on the
side of David and saved him again and again from the hand
of Saul.

By rationalising we can neglect our families, cheat on
our spouse, mount up debts, do the most ego-centric and
selfish deeds. When challenged we try giving plausible reasons for our actions. Like Saul we even pass the responsibility on to God. 'God told me' we say. That approach closes
further argument. It leaves the listener frustrated and the
perpetrator feeling smug and satisfied with himself. A young
girl once told me she was leaving her job because God had
told her to do so. When I queried the wisdom of such an
action, she reiterated that God had told her to do it. The
truth of the matter was that she was not happy in her job or
getting on well with her fellow workers, but to admit this
would have been to lose face.

A man I once knew was very sensitive to any hint of
rejection. He would avoid any meeting in which he could be
criticised, or held to account, because it made him feel as if
he was being rebuffed or put down. He somehow managed
to paint over his avoidance games with a gloss of reasonableness. He had to go to the dentist, or the doctor.
Whatever it was, he would find he had something more
important than the scheduled meeting. One church leader I
heard of managed to change his church council meetings
into prayer meetings and so avoid any uncomfortable dis-
cussions on important issues, which he couldn't handle.
Prayer meetings sounded so much more spiritual than mun-
dane business meetings.

Richard Dortch rationalised about the exciting work of
Heritage USA, and all that the Bakkers were achieving. He
wrote, 'I became so intoxicated with the growth of Heritage
USA, so enamoured with what was developing around me

that I refused to see what was happening.'[16] He rationalised that the project he was involved in was so wonderful that it wasn't worth dealing with the little cracks appearing.

A clergyman was recently reported in the newspaper as having been suspended for adultery. Apparently he had been having an affair with a woman in his congregation, even though he was married with three grown-up children. The woman's husband uncovered the affair by accident because his wife had not shut down the computer and all the emails from her lover were still there. The vicar frequently mentioned God in the messages to her, as if he was trying to persuade himself that God was giving consent to the relationship. In one email he actually used the cross to excuse his behaviour. 'Is marriage meant to be a cross, a lifelong cross dutifully and sacrificially born to satisfy the moralists? Surely the cross of Jesus is there to release us from that kind of bondage, and, if it isn't, then what was the point of his death? What was the meaning of his resurrection if not to set us free to begin again.'[17] The man was self-deceived. By rationalising his actions he could kid himself and the woman concerned that God was on their side, and therefore what they were doing was not sinful.

'Many people,' writes Laura Schlessinger, 'attempt to validate adultery with the belief that it is permissible for a higher cause. People have countless rationales for setting aside the moral implications of their act; for example:

- I love my wife and children and do not want a divorce, so it is better that I have an affair for the sake of my family.
- My husband is not fulfilling me sexually, so it is okay to find sexual satisfaction instead of divorcing my husband.
- I think my husband is being unfaithful, so there is nothing wrong with me having an affair.
- I wasn't looking for an affair – it just happened.
- We are soul mates. etc.

All these rationalisations are attempts to transform an immoral act into acceptable behaviour.'[18]

Wanting peace at all costs and thinking we can get away with it are two of the reasons we live with deception. Both motives are basically self-serving, as are those discussed in the next chapter.

Chapter Five

MESSING WITH THE TRUTH

'The wisdom of the prudent is to give thought to their ways,
but the folly of fools is deception.'
(Prov. 14:8)

Some of the most uncomfortable emotions are shame, embarrassment and a feeling of worthlessness. We all desire to feel good about ourselves and to look good in other people's eyes, in fact these needs are often so pressing that we will mess with the truth in the process of trying to meet them.

SELF-PROTECTION
Most of us are far too self-protective to welcome other people's observations about our behaviour and to own the faults that have been pointed out. Nor are we very good at honestly assessing ourselves. So instead we resort to the age-old strategy of blaming other people when things go wrong.

Scapegoating
This strategy is one of the commonest forms of self-deception and self-preservation. It is a way of avoiding uncomfortable truth about ourselves that we would rather not face. It is usually utilised by people with a low self-esteem, because admitting to being wrong would be too painful and would dent their sensitive image even more. On the other hand people who have an inflated view of themselves, who

have never learned to be self-critical, or honest about their own shortcomings, tend to place blame elsewhere, for the simple reason that they cannot believe they could be in the wrong.

A young man complained to his pastor that he was being persecuted for his faith. When asked to explain he said that he had been sacked from his job. 'Did they say it was because you were a Christian?' His pastor enquired. 'No,' he replied, 'but it has to be that.' It turned out that this was not the first time he had had his employment terminated. In fact he had never had a job for more than six months, before he would be asked to leave. Several people had tried to help him to face whatever was wrong with his attitude, but his only response was to blame his employers. He seemed unable to look at himself, his imperfections and how he was upsetting his bosses.

On many occasions we have tried to counsel married couples whose relationship is floundering. Usually they begin by blaming each other for the failure. But it is only as they both take responsibility for their part in the breakdown, that there is any hope of repair. A common scenario is that as soon as one of them seems to feel the pain of the deteriorating relationship s/he starts to nag the other to 'do something'. Then the partner reacts to being nagged and becomes withdrawn and uncommunicative. Maybe it's a wife who blames her husband for being so useless and passive and he counters by blaming her continual harassment for his lack of co-operation. Whichever way it is the blaming does not lead to a happy outcome.

The only way we resolve these difficult situations is when we take our courage in both hands and ask ourselves the painful questions, 'Is it something I am doing wrong? Do I need to change?' When we begin to take responsibility for our part of the problem, then we are near to finding the solution. This does not relieve the other party of any responsibility – others are accountable for their lives and we for ours. It is true that we can never change another person, only ourselves. Therefore the work to be done is to examine our part in the breakdown and what we can do to start fixing it.

SILENT LIES

The desire to be popular is very strong and at heart we all have a little of the 'people pleaser' in us. At times this 'need' takes precedent over our standards of right and wrong. Silent lying is when we choose to stay silent even when a situation needs confronting. Rather than be different or unpopular we say nothing. A serious failing when we consider Edmund Burke's observation: 'The only thing necessary for the triumph of evil is for good men to do nothing.'[1]

I was recently sent a copy of a speech Charlton Heston, the actor and conservative activist, made at Harvard Law School Forum. In it he told a story of an experience he had had:

> . . . A few years back I heard about a rapper named Ice-T who was selling a CD called 'Cop Killer' celebrating ambushing and murdering police officers. It was being marketed by none other than Time/Warner, the biggest entertainment conglomerate in the World. Police across the country were outraged. Rightfully so – at least one had been murdered. But Time/Warner was stone-walling because the CD was a cash cow for them, and the media were tiptoeing around it because the rapper was black. I heard Time/Warner had a stockholders meeting scheduled in Beverly Hills. I owned some shares at the time, so I decided to attend. What I did there was against the advice of my family and colleagues. I asked for the floor. To a hushed room of a thousand average American stockholders, I simply read the full lyrics of 'Cop Killer'– every vicious, vulgar, instructional word.

I GOT MY 12 GAUGE SAWED OFF. I GOT MY
HEADLIGHTS TURNED OFF. I'M ABOUT TO
BUST SOME SHOTS OFF. I'M ABOUT TO
DUST SOME COPS OFF . . .

It got worse, a lot worse. I won't read the rest of it to
you. But trust me, the room was a sea of shocked,
frozen, blanched faces. The Time/Warner executives
squirmed in their chairs and stared at their shoes.
They hated me for that. Then I delivered another
volley of sick lyrics brimming with racist filth, where
Ice-T fantasizes about sodomizing two 12-year-old
nieces of Al and Tipper Gore. 'SHE PUSHED HER
BUTT AGAINST MY . . .' Well, I won't do to you
here what I did to them. Let's just say I left the room
in echoing silence.

When I read the lyrics to the waiting press corps, one
of them said, 'We can't print that.' 'I know,' I replied,
'but Time/Warner's selling it.' Two months later,
Time/Warner terminated Ice-T's contract. I'll never be
offered another film by Warner, or get a good review
from *Time* magazine . . .

We might say to ourselves, 'Oh, well Charlton Heston is a
rich man anyway and has already made a name for himself.
What did he have to lose?' There is always something to
lose. His stand did not please everyone and he lost some of
his popularity and may be even some work opportunities.

WHITE LIES

Most of us have practised the art of telling white lies. We do
it to cover up silly mistakes, our ignorance or to look good.
I remember many years ago meeting a young missionary
who was very impressive. He told us about his family in
Europe who sounded like royalty. One was a Count and

others were wealthy, important people. Soon after we met someone from the same organisation and happened to mention the young man and his connections. We were amazed to discover that none of it was true. He was just trying to impress us.

No one wants to displease or disappoint others and for this reason most of us have, at sometime, stupidly said we would do something and then not managed to get around to it. We would probably not consider procrastination a lie – we just got our timing wrong. In most cases that might be so, but there are people who consistently put things off. Instead of being honest and saying they haven't the time to do what is being asked, they agree to do it knowing in their heart that it won't get done on time. It is very hard to live or work with a procrastinator. The DIY man who starts a job and every weekend says he will finish it and never does! The friend who says she will return the book, the article of clothing, or the sugar she borrowed and then never remembers! The boss who promises to look into the pay rise, but never gets back to you! The builder who says the job will take six months but is still in your house after nine! The truth is always preferable, even when it is disappointing.

John Newton, the famous hymn writer had many of his letters published. Though written in the rather stilted style of the eighteenth century, nevertheless they are a rich source of wisdom. One is headed 'Some blemishes in Christian character'. He proceeds to name different types of Christians. One he calls 'Volatilis', who is a person who makes promises that he fails to keep. 'Perhaps he is equally sincere in all his promises at the time of making them; but for want of method in the management of his affairs, he is always in a hurry, always too late, and has always some engagement upon his hands with which it is impossible he can comply: yet he goes on in this way, exposing himself and others to continual disappointments.' . . . 'But,' writes John Newton, 'he would do well to remember, that the truth is a sacred thing, and ought not to be violated in the smallest matters . . .'²

Self-protection is a strong motive for lying. When I insisted to the man at the vicarage door that he had not got me out of bed, when we had actually been having a lie in, it was a white lie. I told it to protect my image and I excused it by telling myself that it didn't hurt anyone. The fact that God reminded me of it in such an inconvenient way made me realise that even if I look upon white lies as unimportant, he doesn't.

FEELING GOOD AND LOOKING GOOD!

The following strategies are employed either to 'look good' in other people's eyes, or to 'feel good' about oneself. It would be a surprise if, at some time in our lives, we haven't all employed at least one of these ploys. But because everyone does 'it' at one time or another, doesn't make it right. Especially when Jesus has specifically encouraged us to make our 'yes', 'yes' and our 'no', 'no'.³

Manipulation

This is the art of imposing our will on other people, without them realising it, for the sole purpose of causing them to believe something or do something, which in the end benefits us not them. Os Guinness mentions a *People* magazine report about a certain multimillionaire businessman who choked up while making a speech to lay off some of his workforce. Afterwards everyone was debating whether he was faking it. The magazine's comment was, 'He's a man of disarming charm, his signature bow tie and his grin a little lopsided. The question is, is his warmth real or simply another designer choice?'⁴ Manipulative people can use emotion with great effect.

In the USA there is a plethora of tele-evangelists. One or two of these are past masters at using emotion to sway their audience. A while ago I heard a Christian preacher who spoke with enormous passion. At one stage he had to stop to choke back the tears. I had sat there feeling very uncomfortable and wondering why he was becoming so emotional. Certainly the content of his talk didn't warrant that much ardour. But then I remembered another speaker who had spoken with equal passion, who had touched me deeply. I asked myself why was I comfortable with the one and uncomfortable with the other? Both were very emotional – what was the difference? I came to the conclusion it was to do with integrity. I felt one man's emotion was manipulative and directed towards obtaining an effect from his audience, while the other man's feelings were focused on the subject of his talk, rather than on creating an effect.

We can all be guilty of manipulation. It is an easy trap to fall into in order to make an impression or get our own way. When we want our husband to get on with the DIY he has been promising to do for the last year, we may turn on the tears, hoping it will force him to perform. Or we want to impress our friends and so we exaggerate a story so much that it ceases to bear much resemblance to the actual event. We excuse ourselves because everyone does it. But slowly we find we are living in a world where truth is being sacrificed and we don't know whom to trust. Truth matters supremely because in the end without it there is no freedom. Living in truth is the secret of living free.[5]

However, let's not fall into the other trap of mistaking ordinary persuasion for manipulation. In many situations it is perfectly reasonable to use persuasion to get something done. For example, when I am baby-sitting my grandchildren, I might persuade one of them to go to bed on time, by promising a story, or a treat the next day. I might even use Mum and Dad's reaction to finding them still up when they arrive home, to encourage them bed-wards. This sort of coercion is done for another person's benefit, whereas manipulation only benefits the person using it.

Using Truth

We utilise many strange techniques in our need to look good. We can even make the truth itself serve this purpose. We can mislead others by telling the truth, but not the whole truth. Or by telling the truth in such a way as to leave people believing a lie. When I was at school I envied the children whose fathers were farmers. In my mind to live on a farm would have been the next best thing to paradise. We did in fact live in the country, with a farm just up the lane and we owned a field, an orchard and stables where we kept our horses. Nevertheless my Dad was not a farmer! But I remember occasionally talking, quite truthfully, about the horses, chickens and turkeys we owned, but in such a way that I am sure some thought that I lived on a farm, which was just what I wanted them to think!

Sincerity, candour or intimacy can all be utilised in the effort to impress. A man may tell the story of a personal conversation he had with his son leaving the listener touched by the close relationship between father and son, when in reality, the conversation was the first in months and the relationship was a very poor one. Or, as I heard the other day, a person complains that another person has said something very hurtful, but has only reported half the conversation. She was making it sound much more negative than it really was. In fact the first part of the conversation was very positive, but those comments had not been mentioned and people were left with a false impression. Some people are past masters at using truth to their advantage. President J. F. Kennedy was particularly good at using candour in lieu of truth. Apparently people would walk away thinking they had been told the truth. But, in fact, they had really been told nothing of importance. The small and candid moments set up the big lie.[6]

Stephen Covey says that integrity means avoiding any communication that is deceptive, full of guile, or beneath the dignity of people. He says that 'A lie is any communication with intent to deceive.' Whether communicating with words or behaviour, our intent cannot be to deceive if we have integrity.[7]

It is possible to manipulate a desired response from people by feeding them the sort of information that will lead them to draw the conclusions we want from them. The rest of the data we withhold, knowing that that may lead them to give us advice we don't want to hear. For example those closest to us may tell us that we need to cut down on our commitments. Perhaps we are looking tired, are always in demand and never seem to have time to visit friends or family. But if saying 'no' is very difficult, or we have a need to be needed, then we may be reluctant to tender our resignation and give up one of our commitments. Instead we decide to get some advice from a person who is completely outside the situation. Then it is all too easy to describe one's life in such as way as to make our lifestyle sound perfectly reasonable. In fact we could even make our family sound irrational and selfish.

This is the reason it is so important when trying to help a couple whose marriage is in trouble, to see them both together. So often I have heard only one side of the story and felt quite incensed at the description of the absent spouse's behaviour. But the picture has changed significantly when I have heard the other side. Very few people will repeat a story in which they come off badly. Most of us will paint a picture in our own favour – at least until the hurt and anger has died down. Only then may we view it from a slightly more balanced perspective.

The need to do and say things that satisfy us, make us look intelligent, good or important, is always present, especially in a world where our worth is so often measured by our accomplishments. But however common it is, stretching the truth erodes our conscience and leads us away from facing reality.

Unreality or Insincerity

I once went to speak to a women's meeting that was run by a rather elegant lady. She greeted me as if I was her long lost friend and was so effusive I felt quite embarrassed. After I had spoken she praised me in a way that made me wonder if she might have been listening to someone else. However, I was prevented from getting bigheaded when I heard her thank the ladies who had prepared the very plain ploughman's lunch. The adjectives she used were the same as she had used to describe my talk. It was a new experience to be put in the same category as Cheddar cheese and a roll! For some reason the lady had developed this 'act' over the years and couldn't hear how unreal she sounded. It would have helped her to listen to herself on a tape recording.

Insincerity is an easy trap to fall into when we want to impress those around us.

It can have serious consequences when it is used to offer to others more than one can, in reality, give. When I was about eighteen I worked for a while in a large office building with its own canteen. Every lunchtime I would eat there with my friends. After a few weeks I noticed a young man who continually stared at me throughout the lunch hour. He eventually joined our table and we began to chat together. He was a very friendly man about ten years my senior. I was extremely flattered by his attention and when he asked me out for a drink one evening I readily accepted. Being rather innocent and freshly out of boarding school, I was a little surprised by the overt affection he showed me on a first date. But I was in for a much bigger shock when he casually told me he was married, and that his wife didn't mind him seeing other women. He was suggesting a relationship that he had no right to offer.

Some offer more than they can give quite deliberately, but it is also possible to do it out of sheer carelessness, maybe with the intention of sounding loving and generous, but not meaning to hurt the other person. Very extrovert, affectionate people are not always aware of the signals they are sending to others. Lonely individuals can have their hopes raised by the friendship they think is being offered. Then when they discover that they are just one of many, and their new found friend doesn't really have time for more than a passing relationship, there is a sense of betrayal and disappointment. It is easy for a similar scenario to occur in a counselling relationship, or prayer ministry situation. The person ministering may be a very caring individual, who genuinely has the interests of the other at heart, but is unaware that the needy person, who is hungry for affection, takes the apparent offer of availability literally. This is a good reason for anyone involved in this type of ministry to have some form of supervision.

Some people are unreal simply to keep others at a distance. In the past leaders of churches were discouraged from making close friends within their congregation, and so many developed this rather pseudo self which served as a barrier between themselves and their people. Sadly, because the leader is a model, the people followed suit and were often superficial in their dealings with one another. This unreal manner may be cultivated for the specific purpose of keeping others at arm's length, or it may be just a screen erected to keep a person from having to face an uncomfortable reality. Sometimes people have so many unresolved issues in their lives that they tend to live very carefully, walking on tiptoe as if afraid of disturbing what lies behind the façade.

I heard of a film star who refused any parts which could remind her of her very painful childhood. She had too many rats in the cupboard that she was afraid would be disturbed. Only after she had received some therapy and had learned to deal with her past could she explore more demanding roles. People with unfinished business from the past consistently avoid a situation that might upset their carefully maintained equilibrium. One often hears of a marriage that has gone through a sticky patch because one partner has received some counselling and as a result has changed. One would think that any change for the better in one's partner would be welcomed. But it may be perceived as a threat to the status quo. Suddenly the unchanged spouse finds him/herself living with a real, breathing, hurting person who is sincerely trying to deal with issues in his life, and no longer running away from them. This can be very frightening for a spouse who has not yet found the courage to look behind the screen.

Another reason for projecting a pseudo self is the fear that behind that persona there is nothing – at least nothing worth knowing. One young girl confided in me that she was scared because she sometimes felt like two people, the outside person who looked fine, and the inside person who felt so weak and small. She had a history of horrendous abuse, and it was as if her real self had gone into hiding. Part of her fear was the thought that maybe she had deserved the ill treatment, and that she really had been a stupid, silly thing. So she hid behind an image, afraid of facing the truth about herself, or being mocked by others.

These are some of the infinite ways we devise for avoiding the truth or playing games with it. In this post-modern age with its skewed attitude to truth, the question we must ask ourselves is how much have we bought into the spirit of the age? Is it possible for us to redress the balance, at least in our own lives, and if so how? Given our propensity for self-deception, perhaps we will never live a life of complete dedication to truth. Nevertheless it behoves us, as God's children, to do all that is possible because, the truth is precious and Jesus said that the truth would set us free.[8]

Chapter Six

ALARM BELLS!

'Those things that hurt, instruct.'
(Benjamin Franklin)

When we have reached the point of acknowledging that transformation is part of God's plan for our lives, we have recognised that we are only too capable of deceiving ourselves, and we have decided to challenge this tendency, what next? First we should remind ourselves that 'apart from God we can do nothing'.[1] God is 100% on our side and is vitally concerned with our transformation. If we ask him he will lead us into the truth about ourselves. It is like taking a journey to a strange place – we are more likely to find the way with someone alongside to help us spot the sign posts to our destination.

A good place to start would be to amplify and personalise King David's prayer when he asks God to search him and know him. So we could pray something like: 'Please, dear God, show me what is in my heart. Do I have needs for security and significance that are causing me to avoid the truth, or misuse it for my own benefit? Show me the thoughts that are motivating me and driving me to use deceptive ploys. Alert me to anything in my life that needs attention. Help me to live a transformed life according to your kingdom values and standards of truth.'[2]

It is not beyond the realms of possibility that God will use a supernatural visitation to show us aspects of our lives that need attention. However, it is more likely that he will use ordinary everyday events. All we need are ears to hear the alarm bell ringing and eyes to see it flashing. It's a case of developing a mindset which is determined to overcome our bias towards self-deception and which decides to take notice of the signals that would alert us to the fact that something is wrong. Unless we develop this sort of self-conscious awareness we simply repeat self-defeating behaviour patterns over and over, and then get confused when we reap negative consequences.

I recently had a conversation with a man who had lost his job and been out of work for some time. This was apparently not a one-off experience. He had been given the sack at regular intervals throughout his working life. His marriage had also failed and now he found himself in a lonely and baffled state. He had applied for a new job and his prospective employers asked him to see a psychologist for an assessment. He told me he didn't really understand what the psychologist had said, but it was something to do with him not being able to accept reality. 'Somehow,' he said, 'I seem not to be able to see things as they really are. Perhaps I am protecting myself from the truth. Maybe because it's too painful or threatening.' He asked me to pray for him. I prayed that he would have the courage to drop his self-protective avoidance tactics, and take a good look at himself, because I knew that unless he developed an understanding of himself history was likely to repeat itself. '50 percent of the solution to any problem lies in defining the problem.'[3]

If it is true that, because of our propensity for self-deception, we need God to alert us to aspects of our lives that need attention, what should we be noticing?

REPETITION

Anything negative which repeats itself more than three times could be worth looking at more closely, by asking ourselves some pertinent questions such as: 'Has this happened coincidentally or is there a common thread running through these incidents which could indicate something amiss? If so, what is the common factor and what does it tell me?'

Dreams

Repeated dreams which have familiar feelings, or similar features might be God's way of prompting our unconscious to deal with some unfinished business. I remember for years having a dream that repeated every few months. Though the setting always changed the circumstances were similar and the feelings engendered were the same. I would be in a house searching for a room where all my belongings were kept. Time would be running out but I could never find the room. Every corridor I would draw a blank. I'd wake up feeling tense and anxious. As long as I could remember I had had this type of dream, until I went through a period of 'inner healing'. During that time I resolved many issues that for years had been like 'rats in the cupboard'. As a result I began to experience a sense of wholeness which I had never imagined possible. Significantly, and to my relief, after that the dream ceased and it has never come back. With hindsight I realise that the dream was just one of the ways my unconscious was alerting me to a lack of integration in my life.

A lady once asked me to pray with her because for no apparent reason she had begun to have vivid dreams to do with her father. The backdrop to the dream would always vary but the common factor was the presence of her father. It was as if he was intruding into her mind and demanding some sort of attention. She always woke feeling very disturbed, partly because her father had died the previous year, and she thought she had put the trauma of the loss behind her. As we prayed together a number of unresolved issues to do with her parents, and in particular her father, surfaced. These were all painful experiences that she had buried and then forgotten they had ever happened. It was as if, in her dreams, those incidents were knocking on her conscious mind begging for a resolution. Once in the open she was able to bring the incidents to an appropriate closure. After that she had no more dreams about her dad.

Repetitive Problems

These would appear to be obvious factors for our attention. But it is amazing how many people repeat behaviour that consistently produces negative results, and never stop to ask themselves questions. Our natural inclination for peace and our dislike of disturbance will always put pressure on us to avoid the discipline of self-examination. But unless we grit our teeth and ask ourselves the appropriate question, 'Why does this problem keep re-occurring?' we will never reap the benefit of seeing our actions in a true light, and finding a way of doing things differently.

It's too easy and too tempting to wriggle out of responsibility for problems and place the blame on other people. It's the lazy way out. In that way we can avoid having to make any changes. So parents may blame the school for their child's bad behaviour. Every year the child has a change of class and teacher, but his or her behaviour doesn't improve. Still the parents insist it is the school's fault. To turn the tables on themselves would be very difficult because it could mean having to make some radical changes in their parenting and the type of care they were providing for their child. But until we are prepared, in any repetitive situation, to ask courageous questions of ourselves nothing will change.

With the use of rationalisation we can avoid facing the real cause of our problems for many years. A middle-aged man never stayed long in one job. After a few years he would move on. The reason was always similar. He would find the person in authority over him hard to work with. For years he first made the excuse that he was looking for better opportunities, then he began to blame his work environment for having to move on. Eventually after years of this repetitive behaviour he admitted that he had a problem. He asked for help in finding the reason for his irrational conduct. The first thing that emerged was that the person with whom he had the problem was always male. If the office had both males and females, he only had trouble with the men, and then only if they were senior to him. He tentatively began to take off his blindfold and allow his behaviour to come into focus. He realised that all his life he had been frightened of being rejected by older men. His longing to please them put a strain upon him, and as a consequence he would perform badly. His fear and his shame would become unbearable and eventually he would leave, only to repeat the same scenario in his next place of work. Apparently he had never felt that he had pleased his dad and when his father eventually left the home, he blamed himself. The yearning to please and the fear of loss were transferred to every older male who was in a position of authority over him. Without self-awareness this man would be doomed to repeat his behaviour 'ad infinitum'. The awareness won't necessarily change him, but it certainly provided him with a head start towards healing and change.

Repetitive Criticisms

This could be another God-sent alarm alerting us to something in our life needing examination. No one enjoys being criticised. Immediately it has the effect of making us bristle with indignation. But all negative comments are worth listening to, even if they hurt us. Perhaps they are unfounded, or perhaps they have only an element of truth in them. Whichever it is, if we are in the business of changing and growing it's worth considering whether the comments are valid or not. A repetitive comment said to us by more than one person and about the same issue should always be taken seriously. In fact it is worth learning how to field criticisms so that we don't miss the ones that could benefit us.

The first thing to ask oneself is: 'Who said it?' Is it someone whose opinion we value and respect? Secondly, try and
understand the other person. Has he/she a particular axe to
grind? Have they got a particular reason for being sensitive
about the issue they are raising? And thirdly, we must ask
ourselves if we have received negative input about this matter before. Having understood where the criticism is coming
from, next ask the person to explain their complaint more
fully. Listen carefully, even though you may feel by now
that the complaint is totally unwarranted. Lastly thank
them for it and agree to consider what they have said. In this
way the almost inevitable game of ping-pong is avoided. So
often when we are criticised we hit back in some way, and
then the other person adds to what has been said and we
become even more defensive and reinforce our argument;
backwards and forwards it goes. By agreeing to consider
what has been said the other person feels satisfied and each
is given space to think the comments through.

In the opinion of my husband and most of my friends I
have a tendency to become very focused when preparing a
talk or writing a book, but the flip side of this is that I often
suffer from tunnel vision and then miss seeing other points
of view. The comment is not usually said in the form of a
criticism but more as an observation. Then, a number of
years ago I was doing a series of talks based on my book,
Yesterday's Child. In those talks I rather vehemently suggested that no one should send a child under ten to boarding
school. Later following one of the talks a person came up
who had been very upset by my comments. She was a missionary and had had no choice but to send her children
away to be educated. A few months later a teacher in a boy's
prep school who had heard me speaking made a similar
complaint.

Both had axes to grind so I was inclined to dismiss their
comments. On the other hand it had happened twice. Then
I remembered what those closest to me had said about my

tendency to become over focused. With reflection I realised that though I had a point, I had failed to appreciate that there were people who were forced to choose another way and would therefore be offended by my very definite opinions. I realised that I needed to temper my words, put the point across with less condemnation and admit a few exceptions to the rule. Criticism, if we can bear to hear it, can correct some of our distorted thinking.

Negative comments are particularly difficult to receive from those nearest and dearest, though they, of all people, have the best opportunity to observe discrepancies in our lives. I have not met many people who respond favourably to criticisms from their spouse, parents or close friends. However, before we storm off in a huff, it is worth asking ourselves the question. 'Does this person love me?' If the answer is, 'Yes', then destruction is obviously not their objective. Perhaps they actually want to help! If this is so then we must grit our teeth, take a deep breath, and listen to the comments and consider any criticisms seriously. We may find something surprisingly insightful and beneficial. I would consider David my best critic, though I don't always welcome his help immediately. When he makes suggestions about the layout of a book or changes in a talk, my first reaction is to withdraw. Rather like a snail who pulls back into his shell at the hint of danger. I have to remind myself that David is on my side not against me, and his desire is to help me, not hinder me. Then I gradually relax and listen to his comments.

We were recently in a conversation together with a third person for whom we were both feeling concerned. The more this person denied the need for our concern the more adamant I became and eventually I spoke some home truths with extreme frankness. Afterwards David told me that he thought I had spoken too vehemently and by doing so had undermined my argument. I was furious at this and took refuge in my shell. It took me a while, and it was a struggle, to look back at the conversation objectively and recognise the truth behind the criticism. As I thought about it later I realised that my struggle was not really with my husband, but with my loss of face. I felt shamed by my gaff at speaking as I had done, and was angry that David had drawn my attention to it. I would rather have stayed comfortably unaware of my mistake. But then the truth is often uncomfortable and changing is never easy.

A man once came to see us wanting help with his marriage. His wife had for years been telling him he was selfish and not behaving like a good father or husband. He just shrugged off her complaints as those of a nagging wife. After ten years of this she had eventually given him an ultimatum. 'Change or you can leave.' He was shocked, and for the first time took a good look at himself. He had actually had the chance to do something about his behaviour many times, but until that point had refused to listen to her criticism. If he had done so, his selfishness would have stared him in the face. His weekends of golf, late night drinks with friends, climbing holidays on his own were factual indications of his self-indulgence – all at the expense of his family commitments.

Sometimes it takes shock tactics from someone we respect to bring us to our senses. Nathan the prophet was wise when he went to tackle David about his sin with Bathsheba. He presented his criticism in the form of a story. The story was about a rich man who had a very large number of sheep and cattle, and a poor man who had just one ewe lamb who had grown up with him and his children. One day when a traveller came to visit the rich man, instead of taking a sheep from among his own flock to feed the visitor, he took the poor man's little lamb. When David heard the story he was furious and said the man deserved to die and should pay for the lamb four times over. Then Nathan came clean and said to David, 'You are the man!' As Nathan described David's sin to him the full impact of what he had done hit home and he repented deeply.[4] In fact Psalm 51 is a cry to God from David's heart for cleansing and restoration. 'Create in me a pure heart, O God, and renew a steadfast spirit within me. Do not cast me from your presence or take your Holy Spirit from me. Restore to me the joy of your salvation and grant me a willing spirit, to sustain me.'[5]

Repetitive Failures

We recently heard of a church leader who had been asked to leave his church. It seemed a rather drastic move on behalf of the church council and we wondered what the leader had done to deserve such extreme treatment. When we made some enquiries we were told that he was a brilliant man, but very insensitive and had a habit of upsetting people. Then the person added a telling comment, 'It's the story of his life.' It would seem obvious to an observer that the man in question had a problem that needed to be resolved if he was to continue in 'people centred' work. There has to come a moment when he sits down to ask himself, or others close to him, some appropriate questions, such as, 'What am I doing wrong and why does this continually happen to me?'

When we experience repeated physical failure of some sort we are usually pretty quick to visit our doctor. If I fail to hear the telephone or am constantly having to ask my friends to repeat themselves I hope I would eventually draw the conclusion that something could be wrong with my hearing. However, when our failure impugns our character or abilities, either in our professional or in our personal lives, we find it hard to admit that something may be wrong with us. It is then that we utilise some ploy to avoid the truth, such as blaming others or rationalising. We long for the problem to be placed at someone else's doorstep, or to find extenuating circumstances. It takes courage to examine repeated failures and find the common thread running through them. But taking no notice is like ignoring the red traffic lights. We may get away without an accident once or twice, but eventually we will cause a snarl up, which could have been avoided by stopping at the signal point. Not to stop and ask questions is to miss the opportunity that the red light of failure has afforded us of finding out what we are doing wrong, and rectifying it.

Discomfort

During this last year a noticeable bad smell has surfaced in several parts of our town. Many people have complained to the council because the unpleasant odour indicates a problem that urgently needs attention and the council are the people who have the responsibility for dealing with it. As yet, they have not solved the problem. However, we all know that there has to be a cause for the smell and we will agitate until it is corrected.

Discomfort, physical or emotional, has to have a cause, and should be examined. Physical pain is more easily dealt with than emotional discomfort. A doctor or surgeon will make a diagnosis and hopefully will prescribe the correct treatment. But emotional dis-ease is sometimes nebulous and vague; like slippery soap in the bath it's hard to grasp. However it is a signal alerting us to something which is not right. A person who has told a lie, however harmless, will usually suffer momentary discomfort after the words have left their lips. Someone who has repressed a memory of a bad road accident will usually suffer unusual unease at the mention of a traffic pile up. Similarly sexual abuse victims are frequently unhappy at any mention of sex, and even more uncomfortable and frigid in the marriage bed. Discomfort acts like the bad smell. It is an indication of something wrong which has been buried and is now trying to force itself into our awareness so that we do something positive about it.

Dr Philip McGraw tells the story of a woman who had been sexually abused by her grandfather throughout her childhood and early adolescence. Consequently physical intimacy with her husband had been virtually impossible throughout their marriage. Her grandfather's emotional hold on her was so strong that every time she thought of him, or any man, it brought back unpleasant feelings. She attended one of McGraw's seminars and worked hard on the issues arising out of the abuse. She told the doctor that she felt as if she was locked in a dark, cold room; small and alone and scared. Her discomfort drove her to find a way out of that dark place. Her fear and paralysis were devastating. But she kept moving; she kept slogging her way through – believing that this was her time and her turn. The journey took her through some dark passageways that contained not imaginary but real monsters, but she eventually found the place of freedom that had eluded her for so many years.[6]

Depression

There are many causes for depression but when there is no history of it and no obvious reason for it, then the depression might be a sign of something painful which has been pushed out of sight, but like that 'bad smell' needs to be resolved. One lady I met had had a feeling of unease for several months. She said it was a gloomy feeling without any conscious cause. It gradually worsened and became so bad that she eventually visited a psychiatrist. He asked questions about her family life, but nothing in her past seemed to be an obvious reason for her disquiet. He prescribed some anti-depressants and continued to see her at intervals and continued to dig into her history, but could find no cause for the depression. She told me that one day she was sitting in the doctor's surgery waiting to see him when it was as if a door in her mind opened and she knew exactly why she had been feeling so depressed. It was as if her sub-conscious mind had known the truth all the time, but because it was uncomfortable she had pushed it outside the periphery of her awareness. The truth, she now faced was that her husband was having an affair. Because of this knack we all have for disregarding issues that would cause us pain, she had prevented herself from seeing the truth, but eventually the discomfort could not be ignored.

Anxiety

Even though anxiety may be vague and comes with no label, it is always present for a reason. Asking God to reveal the cause, giving oneself permission to look, and spending time waiting, will usually yield the reason for the anxiety. Once the worry has been brought out into the open and named it is more manageable because we then have some choices. We may decide on some course of action, and just the decision to do something will put our minds to rest. Or perhaps there is nothing we can do except lay it out before God and then leave it in his hands, and repeat this every time the anxiety surfaces. A short time ago I was preparing for bed when I began to feel some disquiet. I lay in the bath and began to search my mind for the cause. At first it eluded me, but as I went through my day I remembered a conversation I had had with a friend while out shopping. She had told me about a common acquaintance who had just had a miscarriage. It had been a very passing remark and I had promptly forgotten it – or so I thought! I had rushed on to do my shopping and the day's events had overtaken me. But as I relaxed the words came back and I realised that her comment had sown a seed of anxiety in my mind for one of our daughters who was expecting a baby. There was little I could do right then except pray, and make a decision to ring her the next day to check all was well. I have learned never to ignore that sort of disquiet. Worry is a thief! It robs us of our peace, our sleep, and probably shortens our lives. In the task of 'knowing ourselves' we have to understand our particular weaknesses, and find ways of tackling them. Worry is one of mine and over the years I have become more adept at managing it and not allowing it to fester unattended.

Change and growth are imperative for a Christian, and God will use an assortment of methods to facilitate this. Self-awareness is the key. Without it we will never change. God will use a variety of means to open our eyes to the inconsistencies in our lives that need dealing with.

Chapter Seven

GOD'S TESTING

'For you, O God, tested us; you refined us like silver.'
(Ps. 66:10)

I recently paid a visit to my brother-in-law Terry's work-shop. In his retirement he restores old furniture. The work-bench was a clutter of bits and pieces in the process of being cut, shaped, fitted and polished. To one side there were several parts of worn out and damaged furniture waiting for attention, and there were also one or two finished articles looking as good as new. It might take him six months, or more, but my brother-in-law will work away until a piece looks like the original in all its elegance. As I looked around that workshop I was reminded of the way God works upon us so painstakingly. He may start with damaged goods, but gradually he begins putting us together bit by bit, with the aim of recreating a person who can once again reflect the image of his creator. God particularly wants a people of integrity. King David said: 'I know, my God, that you test the heart and are pleased with integrity.'[1] David knew what it was to be tested by God through hardships, failures, and betrayals, but in the end the testing bore the good fruit of integrity.

To remake his piece of furniture Terry utilises every available means. He spends hours at car boot sales and antique fairs, searching for just that little piece of wood, brass handle, corner piece, which will exactly match the damaged or missing item at home. Or he buys a new tool that will fashion the wood to its correct specification. Then there is the special polish that produces the beautiful finish. In the same way God utilises every means to fashion his people into his likeness. But we are not inanimate objects like chairs. We are human beings with free will and God is not about to usurp that, even for the infinitely worthy purpose of making us whole. God wants our voluntary co-operation. Therefore in order for us to join forces with him in this objective we have to comprehend the nature of the damage needing repair and healing. For this reason God tests us!

God does not do this to punish us as sometimes we mistakenly think. Nor because he needs to know what is wrong with us – he already knows everything there is to know about us. No, the testing is for our sake, so that we can have insight and awareness into the impurities in our lives so that we can co-operate with God in flushing them out. It is only too easy to live out the whole of our life completely blind to the flaws that mar us. Others may have noticed these, as we notice theirs, but we can easily remain ignorant of our own, unless God opens our eyes. Our lives lack integrity while we remain blind to our inconsistencies. God uses different methods to gain our attention, because he knows he will only have our co-operation if our eyes are opened so that we are faced with reality.

A short while ago a woman sat in our sitting room in tears. Her husband had threatened to leave her, not because he had found someone else to love, but because he was exhausted by her constant nagging and unloving attitude towards him. For years she had used these tactics to try and change him, and had never stopped to listen to herself. Under the threat of desertion, she was faced with the reality of her behaviour. 'I can't believe I have behaved so badly,' she wept. God had her attention.

CIRCUMSTANCES

I have always found Paul's words to the Romans very comforting when he affirms 'that in *all things* God works for the good of those who love him, who have been called according to his purpose'[2] (italics mine). For our personal good, God uses everything and anything to reveal to us the flaws that need our attention.

Our daily circumstances can tell us a lot if only we have eyes to see – so long as we don't get so immersed in a situation that we lose our objectivity and let our own reactions pass unnoticed. Our response to ordinary events can tell us so much. For example how do we react when something we have been looking forward to is cancelled? A lady recently told me how rejected she feels when she has been invited somewhere and for a perfectly good reason the event is cancelled or postponed. With her rational mind she understands that it is not the other person's fault. But emotionally she is still devastated and for days struggles with a sense of betrayal and being let down. Possibly her over-reaction is a signal that she still has some unhealed pain from the past or that whatever healing she has already received, hasn't yet changed her old thinking patterns. She certainly needs to sit down and ask herself what is going on.

When we first went to South America as missionaries we secretly thought the Missionary Society was quite fortunate to have acquired two healthy, and moderately intelligent young people. It only took a few months of living in a completely new culture for the scum to rise to the surface! We were soon made aware of attitudes in us which were less than godly! We were often impatient and intolerant of the seemingly lackadaisical attitude found in South America. 'Manana' was the 'in' word. Everything, it seemed, could wait until tomorrow. In our pride we thought that we had our priorities in better order. It was hard to accept that perhaps the Chileans were right and we were wrong when they put people and family above punctuality. In general their philosophy of life was much more relaxed and far less driven than was ours. Over the years we came to appreciate their love of family, their attitude to children, and the time they gave to people.

I recently heard a story that graphically illustrated the wisdom of their priorities. A philosophy professor stood before his class with some items in front of him. He wordlessly picked up a large empty mayonnaise jar and proceeded to fill it with rocks right to the top, rocks about 2" diameter. He then asked the students if the jar was full? They agreed that it was. So the professor then picked up a box of pebbles and poured them into the jar. He shook the jar lightly. The pebbles, of course, rolled into the open areas between the rocks. He asked his students again if the jar was full? They agreed that yes, it was. The professor then picked up a box of sand and poured it into the jar. Of course, the sand filled up any remaining space. 'Now,' said the professor, 'I want you to recognise that this is your life. The rocks are the important things – your family, your partner, your health, your children – and anything else so important to you that if it were lost, you would be nearly destroyed. The pebbles are the other things in life that matter, but on a smaller scale. They represent things like your job, your house, your car. The sand is everything else. The small stuff. If you put the sand or the pebbles into the jar first, there is no room for the rocks. The same goes for your life. If you spend all your energy and time on the small stuff, the material things, you will never have room for the things that are truly most important. Pay attention to the things that are critical in your life. Play with your children. Take your partner out dancing. There will always be time to go to work, clean the house, give a dinner party and fix the disposal. Take care of the rocks first – the things that really matter. Set your priorities. The rest is just pebbles and sand.' After living in Chile for a few years we realised that we had been in danger of putting the sand and pebbles – small and unimportant things – first.

So our new circumstances tested our attitudes. Then our trust in God was tested when we experienced our first huge earthquake. I was terrified and desperately wanted to escape the unreliable land of volcanoes and earth tremors. I longed to enjoy the security of England once again. In the panic I forgot about 'God's call'. I just wanted to be safe. During those first five years of our time in Chile, through all the different circumstances, we were being tested. At the time these tests were uncomfortable, sometimes painful, but God used them to show us many things about ourselves we needed to know. We certainly returned home for our first leave wiser and humbler people.

OTHER PEOPLE

In the film *Castaway*, the actor Tom Hanks is shipwrecked on a desert island, and for months on end he is totally alone. The solitude is so unbearable that he invents a companion in the form of a football that he decorates to look like the head of a person whom he calls 'Wilson'. He talks over his day, his plans, and his thoughts with Wilson, and it is probably this invented friend that stops him from losing his mind. In the beginning God said that it wasn't good for man to be alone and normally we need companionship, but occasionally being forced to face ourselves without the buffer of friends and family around can be painfully revealing. So often unrelenting busyness, noise and constant company protects us from ever stopping to take stock of ourselves. It wouldn't hurt us, now and again, to take a solitary retreat in the heart of the countryside and see what we learn about ourselves.

However, while people can distract us from facing some uncomfortable truths, conversely their company can also be God's method of testing us. The first year of any marriage is usually a real eye-opener. One discovers weaknesses one never knew existed until having to share life with someone of the opposite sex, from a completely different background, having distinctive likes and dislikes. One becomes aware of tendencies that only show up in a close relationship. For example a young couple nearly came to blows after just a few months. The husband turned out to be very controlling of his spontaneous young wife. Until living in close proximity to someone with a free spirit, his desperate need to be in control of every situation had never really come home to him. He was wise enough to own that the major part of the problem was his perfectionism, which was his way of trying to make his world a safe place.

For many years a colleague and I have led retreats at a nearby Convent. It was interesting to learn of the Nuns' struggles as they attempted to live in a close community. It reminded me of our own efforts to live peacefully alongside other missionaries. For nearly seventeen years we shared our home with others – sometimes a married couple, other times a single person. Despite the fact that we were all Christians it was not always easy. Sometimes, much to my disgust, disagreeable attitudes, of which I was unaware, would surface in my life. I had always rather prided myself on being patient and long-suffering until I had to share our home with a couple and their small child. The little boy was full of mischief and could wreck the house in seconds. He tried my patience continually. I found it so hard to go the second mile and offer to baby-sit the toddler occasionally to help the mother who wanted to go off and pray. I gained comfort from the words of St James when he encouraged his readers to 'Consider it pure joy, my brothers, whenever you face trials of many kinds, because you know that the testing of your faith develops perseverance. Perseverance must finish its work so that you may be mature and complete, not lacking anything.'[3] But sometimes it felt as if God's testing was over the top! That particular test, of my ability to live peacefully with others, seemed to be constantly targeted, and I was tempted to become resentful.

Then I remembered my days playing tennis at school. Our PE mistress would take us out on to the court and just aim balls at us. Over and over she would aim them at my backhand because that was my weakest stroke, and she wanted to strengthen it. God not only tests us so that we become aware of our weaknesses, but also to help correct those weaknesses and to make us stronger.

SUFFERING

Suffering is part and parcel of our lives here on earth. None of us will escape it in some form or another. However, though I do not believe God deliberately sends it, I firmly believe he permits it and uses it for our benefit. It's just another one of his 'all things'. Perhaps more than anything else hardships show us what is really in us. The only thing that can spill out of a cup when it is knocked is what is already in it. When we have lived a relatively pain free life suffering comes as a shock to the system. The feelings and attitudes that are expressed during that time might never have come to light except for those difficult circumstances. After the terrible tragedy which struck New York on the morning of 11th September 2001, many people sought sanctuary in churches, not for physical safety, but because they sought the reassuring presence of the eternal God of hope. Until terror and uncertainty hit us we are often unaware of the latent insecurity and apprehension hidden within us.

The word 'cancer' raises fear in most hearts. I have many friends and some relatives who have had to come to terms with it. I was particularly impressed recently with a friend who had a very serious battle with cancer. Although the prognosis was poor she had an extremely positive attitude. She attacked the illness with every means available. She received the chemotherapy, she watched her diet very carefully, spent time in prayer, kept in touch with friends who were particularly encouraging and helpful, she put right any relationship that needed repair and decided to celebrate and enjoy fully whatever life she had left. I felt very challenged by her attitude and wondered if I could have been so positive. These painful situations test us, revealing character defects and the quality of the relationship we enjoy with God.

After the boy David was anointed for kingship, he had a long wait before he actually came to the throne. In the period between the anointing and the crowning he suffered severely at the hands of King Saul who sought to kill him. He was hounded from pillar to post and spent most of his time hiding in caves. At least twice he had the opportunity to kill Saul, but he could never find it in him to lift a finger against God's anointed. The bitterness, jealousy and anger that consumed Saul were never exhibited in David's life. The suffering showed David to be a man after God's own heart, fit to lead his people. Saul was shown up as an insecure man, unfit to be king.

Most of us can recognise the above situations as God's way of testing us. We may not see them in those terms at the time, but later, if we will take the time to examine our reactions, we will learn a lot about ourselves. However, God is very creative and there is yet another tool he uses, which is rather unexpected. It is a common everyday experience, which we may never have regarded as a test, but one which could tell us a great deal about ourselves if we cared to stop and take note.

PRAISE

The writer of the Proverbs tells us that the crucible tests silver for impurities and the furnace tests gold, and then he goes on to make a surprising statement. 'Man is tested by the praise he receives.'[4] At first glance it seems improbable that a 'well done' for something we have achieved could test us for flaws in our character. But maybe it isn't the praise itself that shows us anything, *but the way in which we receive it* that may or may not show up some cracks in our lives. Therefore, when we are praised for passing an exam, completing a task, giving a talk, helping out, or listening to a friend, the question we should ask ourselves is: 'How did that make me feel and how did I respond?' Our reaction to praise could be very revealing.

Difficulty Receiving

Some people find it difficult to receive praise. They may find it so hard that the person giving the compliment is left doubting whether or not his or her words have been well received. Instead of accepting the tribute and allowing it to build them up, they put up a wall of defence so that the words don't penetrate. Such people appear rude and thankless, and leave their fans feeling discouraged and put down. The roots of this reaction usually lie in a low self-image and a mistrust of people generally. Low self-esteem causes them to think that they don't deserve or merit good things. In fact they have a lot in common with the anorexic, who besides denying herself good nourishing food, often finds it difficult to receive the benefits of a compliment. In her eyes the person who compliments her must be stupid, or otherwise they would see plainly that she was really an 'awful person'. She feels that she doesn't deserve to be cared for or complimented, believing that she is 'a nothing'.[5] Sadly such a person deprives herself of people's encouragement and affirmation, the very thing which could heal and lift her painfully low self-esteem.

Sometimes painful experiences from the past are still controlling their expectations of people in the present. So they react to admirers if they were as insincere, cruel, or careless as a care-giver or close friend they have had in the past. When the actor, Alec Guinness, was eighty John le Carré wrote an article about him in *The Daily Telegraph*. He described Alec Guinness as an eighty-year-old man with a watching child inside him who had still found no safe harbour. The deprivations and humiliations of three-quarters of a century were still unresolved. Apparently Alec loathed the flattery of the world around him and mistrusted its praise. Sadly the famous actor didn't know that God was able to heal and restore that watching child, and give him back the trust he had once lost.

Pleasure with Anxiety

So there is the 'brick-wall' reaction and then there is the 'pleasure tinged with anxiety' reaction. Some people receive praise in the first instance with pleasure, but this is quickly followed by a sense of apprehension. If you live with the belief that people only value you if you are successful and perform well, then your value always hangs in the balance. Success is never guaranteed to any of us. The possibility of failure is a reality throughout life. If you have been admired for your perfect figure and beautiful hair and skin, then lurking in the back of your mind could be the thought: 'They admire me now, but say if I get fat and wrinkly, will they still think well of me then?' With this thought people's praise is greeted with a mixture of happiness and fear.

A young man once told me that he had had a nervous breakdown while at University and had had to take a year out. He had passed his GCSEs and then his 'A' levels with flying colours and the school, his family and friends had been delighted. Unfortunately the university course he had chosen was more difficult than he had anticipated. He had not got on well with his tutors and gradually he had begun to lose confidence. In fact he feared he was going to fail, not just his course but all those who believed in him. Every time he went home depressed his parents encouraged him and told him how proud they were of him. This made him more anxious than ever. Their praise did nothing to reassure him. In fact it generated panic attacks. The year out enabled him to meet with a counsellor who helped him examine the beliefs he held about himself, his parents, his sense of value, and fear of failure. He realised that because he had succeeded all his life he had never experienced his parents' unconditional love in the midst of failure. Irrationally he had linked his success and their love together. His value had become mixed up with performance and other people's admiration. Little by little he worked at changing his misconceptions. It was as if he had been given a new pair of spectacles with which to see the world. At first it seemed strange but gradually his view of life came into proper focus.

Longing and Depression

Another common reaction is also a mixed one. It starts off as hopeful longing and ends up as depression. This is the reaction of a person hungry for praise. He or she waits for it eagerly, even drops some broad hints but when the longed for compliment comes it somehow isn't enough. However much praise that comes their way it never satisfies, and they are left feeling deflated and empty.

The prolific and popular writer and speaker, the late Henri Nouwen, was such a person. *Wounded Prophet* was an apt title for his biography. As one person wrote of him, 'He got more affirmation than anyone I know' – but, his biographer added, 'It was never enough. The truth that he was loved, not only by his many and most critical of friends, but by the scores of readers who wrote to him every week, seemed to make little difference.' He was a natural actor and audiences would go home inspired and enthralled by what they had heard and seen. However, there were times when the brilliant communicator would go back alone to his hotel room and become the sad clown. It seems that his problems stemmed from his relationship with his father who had been a distant, success-driven man, who had never given his son the affirmation he longed for, leaving Henri with a gaping hole in his heart, which no amount of admiration seemed to fill.[6] It was like filling a bucket with holes in the bottom.

Henri Nouwen's problem is a common one in this

'fatherless generation'. Few growing up today will have had enough affirmation from the important adults in their lives and many are left with an insatiable hunger for love and encouragement. It is a hole in the heart that many try and fill by manipulating others to give them that longed for affirmation, but when given discover it doesn't really satis-fy. In the end it is only God who can fill that vacuum. Though Henri struggled most of his life with unmet needs, he knew the answer to his inner longings and shares it most clearly in his book, *Life of the Beloved*. His problem, com-mon to most of us, was knowing the truth in his mind but not having it embedded in his heart in a way that would make him contented in his everyday life. He wrote to a friend: 'As long as "being the Beloved" is little more than a beautiful thought or a lofty idea that hangs above my life to keep me from becoming depressed, nothing really changes. What is required is to become the Beloved in the commonplaces of my daily existence and, bit by bit, to close the gap that exists between what I know myself to be and the countless specif-ic realities of everyday life.'[7]

Feeding on the Praise

Yet again others receive praise only to feed off it in an unhealthy manner. It's a real temptation for gifted people who are constantly in the limelight and admired by the pub-lic, to become puffed up and big-headed. The problem starts when such a person surrounds himself solely with sycophants. He or she is then in danger of losing contact with reality. Nobody is prepared to bring them back to earth and face them with their fallibility.

However, it isn't just a temptation for the gifted. It can happen to anyone who cannot be bothered to examine his heart, nor ask the Holy Spirit to search him out. It's impor-tant that we learn to receive a compliment graciously. However, if we value integrity, we will learn not to feed off it in an unhealthy way. If we do allow someone's praise to go to our heads it usually means that we have lost touch with reality and have ceased to ask ourselves tough questions. Not only that but if we search further back it usually means that in the beginning there were unmet needs which the admiration was able to tap into. It works a little like a hairdryer. It only functions if the plug is inserted into a socket. Without a socket there is nothing for the device to plug into and it will not work. In the same way, admiration will not go to our heads unless there is a socket of self-doubt or insecurity for the praise to plug into.

Matt Redman is a well-known worship leader who has led thousands into the presence of God. He has written a very helpful little book about worship. One chapter is more designed for those who aspire to lead worship, than the ordinary worshipper in the pew. They are words of wisdom for people who may never be famous, but have a slightly more up-front ministry than others in the church. He says that the toughest test doesn't come when we are alone with no one looking, but when we start getting trusted with the public stuff. 'Maybe that's playing in the worship team at church, or whatever. God calls us to check ruthlessly the motives of our hearts. Do we still want to be unnoticed worshippers now that we're on stage? Or is there a part of us that really wants to be a "noticed" worshipper? Are we still happy to serve? Or is there even just a tiny part of us wanting to be served? Are our songs still aimed at an audience of one, or deep down are we starting to want wider acclaim? These are the tough questions to face, but they're essential if we're going to stay faithful to the calling God has on our lives.' He goes on to ask other difficult questions like – 'and what's going through our minds when we lead? Are there little moments of self-congratulation when things are going well?' 'Praise,' (meaning praise of God), 'is a contradiction of pride. Pride says "look at me", but praise longs for people to see Jesus. There is no room for showing off in the Holy throne room.'[8]

People who are blind to their own weaknesses are dangerous. Without thought such people can find themselves in very compromised situations. There is safety in being able to take a step back and look at oneself objectively. Had Peter been able to do this he might not have denied Jesus. A few days previously Peter had assured Jesus that he would be willing to lay down his life for him. But Jesus knew better! 'Will you really lay down your life for me? I tell you the truth, before the cock crows, you will disown me three times!'9 As Jesus had predicted when Peter was tested he lied to protect himself. If he had truly known himself he might never have put himself into such a dangerous position – like the others he would have kept his distance. Peter came crashing down and reality confronted him in a most painful way. It was this failure that prepared Peter for the work Jesus had for him to do – founding his church. Those, like Peter, who have been humbled, stripped of their pride and know themselves, make more trustworthy co-workers and leaders.

Gratitude and Humility

Lastly there are those who receive praise with gratitude mixed with humility. These are people who benefit from the encouragement, but have a true evaluation of their gifts. Our gifts come from God and without him we can do nothing. So, although it is good to be encouraged and affirmed, because it spurs us on to do more, we know that in a moment God could set us aside. The speaker could lose his voice, the musician could go deaf, the athlete could break a limb and the writer could lose his inspiration.

Life is very whimsical. And the wise person knows that it's foolish to become dependent on admiration in order to feel of value. He also knows the truth, that recognition and admiration can never make him a special person. If the truth were known there are many thousands who quietly go about helping and blessing others whose good deeds will never receive public acknowledgement, but whose reward is yet to come.[10] In fact I have often imagined arriving in heaven and seeing throngs of totally unknown people, who have spent their lives doing good, receiving their crowns – wonderful, glittering tiaras – being the envy of us all. And the many famous people who had received so much adulation here on earth being told they had already received their reward!

The way in which we receive praise can be a mirror if we care to look into it. Our hearts' reaction to being complimented may not be obvious to others, but if we take time to reflect on the feelings which have been stimulated we might be surprised at just what those emotions can tell us. After that it is up to us what we do about what we have learned. The pieces of furniture in my brother-in-law's workshop were inanimate objects without minds and wills. We are animate human beings with the ability to think and make choices. Again and again throughout our lives we will be given opportunities for taking stock and making self-assessments. It is then up to us whether or not we co-operate with God in changing. We can ignore the tests he has allowed to come our way and learn nothing from them, or we can chose to take notice and then take action.

However, it is one thing to know that action is needed and another to take it. Change is difficult and threatening. Without the aid of the Holy Spirit it would seem too much of an uphill struggle. He is involved in opening our eyes to the flaws in our lives – then he stands by to help us towards transformation. The usual way that God works is gradually and silently, through the everyday happenings of our lives. But occasionally he uses a more dramatic method to convict us of our need for change.

Chapter Eight

AWAKENING!

*'But now my eyes have seen you. Therefore I despise myself
and repent in dust and ashes.'*
Job 42:5,6

'Woe to me!' cried the prophet Isaiah. 'I am ruined! For I
am a man of unclean lips, and I live among a people of
unclean lips, and my eyes have seen the King, the Lord
Almighty.'[1] Isaiah had experienced an awakening. He had
suddenly become aware of his sin, and the sin of the people
amongst whom he lived. In particular he realised that he was
guilty of deceit, hypocrisy, lies – the sins of the tongue. His
awakening was a result of a vision of God. He saw God on
his throne, high and exalted and the train of his robe was
filling the temple. The seraphs were there calling to one
another: 'Holy, holy, holy is the Lord Almighty; the whole
earth is full of his glory.'[2]

It was at this point that Isaiah's eyes were opened to the
reality of his true state. Whatever pretence and sham had
existed previously in his life it was all stripped away in that
instance. He felt completely devastated in the light of God's
holiness. His relief must have been immense when the seraph
flew to him with a live coal in his hand and touched his
mouth, saying, 'See, this has touched your lips; your guilt is
taken away and your sin atoned for.'[3]

The sort of awakening that Isaiah experienced is life-
changing. But we may only receive such a revelation once or

twice in our lives. The rest of the time it is a case of co-operating with God, who works away in us, 'little by little'. This
was the experience of the Children of Israel when they
crossed over the Jordan into the Promised Land. God
declared that he would go before them, but that he would
only drive out the nations who were inhabiting the land,
'little by little'. He said that Israel would not be allowed to
eliminate them all at once, or the wild animals would mul-
tiply around them.[4]

God could quite easily have empowered his people to
wipe out the pagan tribes in one day, but in his infinite wisdom he chose to do it over a period of time – though during those years of conquering the land the people of Israel
had many experiences of God's supernatural intervention.
One of the first was at Jericho after Joshua was visited by a
man who introduced himself as the commander of the army
of the Lord. He gave Joshua clear instructions about how to
capture Jericho. And when Joshua obeyed the Lord the walls
of Jericho came tumbling down and the children of Israel
took the city.[5]

Another time the Gibeonites, who had made a covenant
with Israel, requested help from Joshua when they were
under attack from five kings of the Amorites. During the
battle the Lord not only rained down huge hailstones which
killed more of the enemy than the sword but he also caused
the sun to stand still for a full day until the nation had
avenged itself of its enemies. The writer reported that there
had never been a day like it before or since, 'a day when the
Lord listened to a man. Surely the Lord was fighting for
Israel.'[6] From this it would seem that although Israel only
conquered the Promised Land 'little by little', as God had
said, nevertheless he intervened on many occasions in a supernatural way to move them on in their conquest.

In the same way the normal route God chooses to show
us the inconsistencies in our lives and change us, is through
ordinary circumstances. But now and again he intervenes

supernaturally to awaken us to our true state and then we experience significant change in a short space of time

REVIVALS

Supernatural visitations do happen and when they do they are wonderful, never-to-be-forgotten turning points, which bless the recipient and change his life. This has been witnessed down through the years in the many revivals that have occurred. Revivals and awakenings are synonymous – a sleeping church is revived, or wakes up from sleep. As a result there is a heightened awareness of sin and of the presence of a Holy God. People are saved, Christians repent and many are anointed with gifts of the Holy Spirit.

The revival which hit North America in the eighteenth century was called the Great Awakening. One of the men used by God at this time was Jonathan Edwards. When he preached his hearers would come under such conviction of sin that they would cry out and weep loudly. Some would be so overcome that they would fall down. There were many quite strange manifestations during that time. People would receive visions and dreams. Others would fall under the power of the Spirit as if in a faint. Edwards was reluctant to interfere because he observed that many of those who had been affected were lastingly changed. During those days of revival, Edwards said that 'there was as much done in a day or two as at ordinary times is done in a year'.[7]

On one occasion he was preaching in a town called Enfield when the Holy Spirit began to convict the hearers of their sin. 'Suddenly they were overwhelmed and strong men were gripped with the most awful fear of hell, some of them felt they were already slipping down into the fires of a lost eternity and they clung to the pillars of the meeting house and cried for mercy.' The results were lasting.[8] There is no doubt that when God moves in this supernatural way lives are changed. A fear of God comes upon people and holiness is the natural outcome. In fact during the Welsh revival of the early twentieth century the work in the mines came to a standstill because the pit ponies could no longer understand the orders that were given them. The hauliers, who were famous for their profanity and cruelty, were no longer driving the ponies with curses and the animals were confused.[9]

Sadly in normal times Christians are less troubled by bad language, ungodly attitudes and selfish behaviour which does not reflect their so called commitment to a Holy God. They try to get away with secret immorality; they go along with unfair business practices and they lie to save face. But when they experience a personal awakening then suddenly a passion for holiness is born in them. 'Revival is always a revival of holiness. And it begins with a terrible conviction of sin.'[10]

Commenting on the Azusa Street Revival in Los Angeles in 1906, Frank Bartleman says that God broke strong men and women to pieces and put them together again for his glory. It was a tremendous overhauling process. Pride, self-assertion, self-importance and self-esteem could not survive there. He said that, 'Presumptuous men would sometimes come among us. Especially preachers with their self-opinions. But their efforts were short-lived. They generally bit the dust in humility going through the process we had all gone through.'[11]

It reminds one of Job's experience when God finally faced him up with some tough questions that put Job firmly in his place, 'Where were you when I laid the earth's foundations?' he demanded. Or 'Have you ever given orders to the morning or shown the dawn its place?' God left Job speechless, knowing he had no answer. 'Brace yourself like a man,' said God. 'I will question you and you shall answer.' More questions ensued until finally Job found the strength to answer. 'You said, "Listen now, and I will speak; I will question you, and you shall answer me." My ears had heard of you but now my eyes have seen you. Therefore I despise myself and repent in dust and ashes.'[12]

Job had a revelation of God and the result was that he saw himself as he really was, a sinful human being, and he was disgusted with himself.

PERSONAL AWAKENINGS

God uses many ordinary, everyday happenings, such as we have already mentioned, to show up impurities in our lives. But progress is often slow. Now and again we could do with a shake up. Something that would wake us up to the reality of God's holiness, and the unacceptably relaxed attitudes we have about the flaws and inconsistencies in our lives. Just as we need to be filled with the Spirit continually, we need more than one awakening. We need times when we are woken up to the needs of the poor and disenfranchised, or the call of God on our lives, or the plight of the lost, or our lack of holiness. Just recently I was sitting with several thousand others listening to a talk about the cross. Suddenly the preacher was gripped by the awfulness of the cross and at the same time its power to change lives. He spoke with great passion. That morning many people hearing him experienced a personal 'awakening' to the meaning of the cross.

Many years ago, while living in South America, I listened to a tape recording by a lady who was speaking about a time when she had seen herself through the eyes of God and how it had changed her life. Without really thinking of the consequences I thought this sounded like a good idea. So I prayed that I too might see my life the way God saw it. Well, I soon regretted that prayer. In the six months that followed it was as if scales fell from my eyes and I began to see my life with all its carelessness and selfishness. I realised how lax I had become in my relationship with God and my regard for holiness of life. I felt weighed down with how far short I had fallen from my own standards – let alone God's. I confessed my sin to God again, and again, but without any sense of relief. The heavens were silent. I became depressed and wondered whether I would ever feel joyful again. One day I was crying out to God for his help when I suddenly had an 'awakening'. I woke up to the reason Christ died. He was punished by crucifixion for my sin. He died instead of me. I had known this the whole of my Christian life, but I had never felt so desperately in need of it until that moment. Suddenly the cross became the central point of my existence. I saw salvation as a personal necessity, not as a matter of doctrine just to be believed. As God opened my eyes to his provision, I clung to the cross like a drowning person clings to a life raft. For several years after that I could speak of nothing else. Whatever subject I was asked to speak on what they got was the cross and the forgiveness bought for us there. We all need times of 'awakening' like this, when we are brought face to face with the paucity of our lives, the need we have to avail ourselves of God's forgiveness, and to pursue holiness because without it no one will see the Lord.[13]

These times of revival purge us of so much rubbish that accumulates over the years. We can become so inured to the discrepancies and inconsistencies that exist in our lives that we become unaware of how far short we have fallen of God's holiness. But a fresh move of the Holy Spirit will awaken us to our need. A few years ago when the Holy Spirit was moving with unusual power in our church, a young girl made her way down the aisle looking for someone to talk to. She was obviously very upset and was crying so much she could hardly speak. I waited for her to calm down enough to tell me what was wrong. Eventually the sad story came tumbling out. She had been brought up in a strict Catholic home but during her late teens had rebelled against her parents so much that she had run away from home. She ended up living with a variety of men, had twice become pregnant and had had the babies aborted. Four years into her rebellion she was in a real mess. At this point she accepted an invitation to church.

During the evening she had become more and more depressed and desperate. She decided that she must have committed the unforgivable sin, and that she could never be forgiven. I talked to her for a while about the cross and how Jesus had died in her place. She just cried even louder. I asked her to confess her sins aloud and then I pronounced forgiveness over her. But she still didn't seem to be able to lay hold of it, and continued to cry brokenheartedly. For a while I was at a loss how to help her. Then the thought came to me that she needed something tangible to make the truth come alive. So I took her by the hand to the very front of the church where a big wooden cross hung on the wall. It was so big it nearly touched the ground. I asked her to close her eyes, and then to imagine all the sins she had just confessed being placed in her outstretched hands. Then I asked her to lay her hands on the cross. I told her that as she did so those sins would be placed where they belonged, and when she took her hands away her sins would remain on the cross. She did as I suggested. I told her not to take her hands away until she was sure she could leave her sins there. She hesitated for so long that I was afraid she wouldn't be able to do it. Then she took her hands away and as she did so she dropped to the foot of the cross, sobbing with relief and thanksgiving. For that young girl the whole evening had been like an awakening. First to the state of her heart and then to the miracle of God's forgiveness.

RESULTS

One of the results of a supernatural awakening is passion. Suddenly the work of changing is not a hard slog but an exciting challenge – a rewarding task – a goal to be achieved. With passion comes new energy to do the work, and a new vision that feeds the desire to be different. Because of this infusion of passion and energy the normal stages of growth are often concertina-ed, and some stages may even be skipped all together. However, when the gradual process of change takes place certain elements are normally found. With each of us the timetable and sequence may be different, but generally similar factors are present.

- First of all an acknowledgement and owning of the problems which may be hindering growth, and a gradual understanding of the exact nature of those problems.
- After that there may be a period of healing when root traumas are healed. This is only complete when those who have been responsible for the disturbing events are forgiven.
- However, healing of painful memories is not the final goal. The objective has to be greater than this. Our main aim always has to be removal of those hindrances to change and growth.
- The freedom to achieve this finally comes with repentance, when the person recognises the ungodly attitudes and the protective strategies he or she has adopted in order to live with a minimum of discomfort. True repentance always facilitates change, because for the first time there is a real awareness of how far one's life has fallen short of being like Jesus.

When the awakening is a sudden, supernatural occurrence some of the steps that may, in normal circumstances, have taken months, or even years, are rapidly negotiated. Which is a bonus! However, whether it happens suddenly or gradually, at some stage we need to have our eyes opened to the condition of our lives. We cannot continue to live protecting ourselves from the discomfort of self-awareness. For the sake of integrity we need to wake up, one way or another, to the discrepancies we live with so comfortably. It doesn't really matter whether God uses everyday experiences to catch our attention, or whether he uses a supernatural move of the Spirit to do it. It's not really either/or. It is both/and. Whichever it is, the result should be the same – holiness of life.

Chapter Nine

HELP YOURSELF

'To have what you want you have to do what it takes.'[1]

Without a shadow of a doubt we need God's help in our efforts to become self-aware people. He makes us conscious of those inconsistencies which would hinder our becoming holy as he is holy. However, there are practical steps we can take to help ourselves become such people. We have already examined the numerous ordinary ways God uses to catch our attention, as well as the occasional supernatural awakenings when he compels us to face up to the true state of our hearts and awakens a passion for holiness. However, there are certain things we can do to help ourselves become people of integrity, who dare to live open-plan lives, both within ourselves and with others, in the pursuit of holiness.

DEVELOP A MINDSET

We will never bother to examine ourselves, or even notice the discrepancies in our lives if we haven't first decided to do so. At some stage we have to make a decision to become the sort of people who will notice God's nudges, other people's hints, as well as experiences which indicate a need for change. We have to decide to challenge our particular methods of avoiding the truth, which means moving out of our comfort zone. But if it is just a one-off event it will be ineffectual. It has to become a way of life – a habit. Apparently the great educator, Horace Mann, once said that habits are like a cable. We weave a strand of it every day and soon it cannot be broken.[2] It is not quite true because I know that habits can be broken eventually, but it takes time and effort, just as it takes time and effort to make them. We are not talking here of a one-off, good idea, for a short span. It's rather like losing weight and maintaining it. Crash diets are fine just to fit into an outfit for a one-off occasion. But if you want to maintain your weight loss and lead a healthy life, then you have to develop a mindset, which continually thinks low fat, low sugar and exercise.

I have a friend who puts on weight very easily. She goes on a yearly diet. It is always a starvation diet that rewards her with amazing results, and ecstatic visits to the scales. Then for about two months she is happy and determined. But as her size decreases so too does her determination. She grows lazy and begins to enjoy the pizzas and the Mars Bars once again. For such a person there is only one answer. She needs to set herself a healthy diet that she observes for the rest of her life. Leading a self-conscious life, in the right sense, has to have a similar mindset. We have to make a decision to live our lives 'noticing' – noticing how we relate to others; noticing our ups and downs; noticing our feelings; our thought processes; our behaviour. Having the right mindset is important. But of itself it is not enough. We have to be pro-active and take positive steps to know ourselves better.

The fact is you may be the person you know least about. Yet you are the person with whom you spend the most time; you are the person in whom you have the most invested. So you must not underestimate the gravity and importance of getting to know yourself.[3]

Personality Analysis Tests

If self-awareness is the road to integrity, then anything that opens our eyes to our motives, attitudes, thought processes, defence mechanisms, and behaviour, is worth pursuing. Two helpful aids to self-knowledge are the Myers Briggs, and the Taylor Johnson personality analysis tests. Myers Briggs helps us to identify our personality type.[4] The Taylor Johnson is particularly helpful in showing up our strengths and weakness. For me personally the Taylor Johnson was the most insightful, and sparked the most change in my life. I did it many years ago while attending a CWR[5] counselling course, led by Selwyn Hughes. We were given the option of doing the test. I thought I might as well, though I honestly thought it would only reveal what a balanced person I was! When the results came back I was shocked. Several areas were marked as needing attention. At first I couldn't believe my eyes. So I asked to have the paper re-checked. Back it came as correct. So I was forced to take a serious look at myself. Looking back now I see that that uncomfortable 'moment of truth' was responsible for propelling me into a time of significant growth and change, for which I will always be thankful.

There are several books with exercises that will help us to know ourselves better. *Your Personality and the Spiritual Life* by Reginald Johnson contain questions designed to help people understand their personality according to the Myers Briggs typing.[6] *The Secret of Staying in Love* by John Powell[7] is aimed at helping married couples, or friends grow in intimacy. But the questions could be done equally well alone in the interest of self-awareness. However, in case none of these books are available to the reader, I have listed below some questions that might help you to know yourself better. But before attempting them it is important to understand our likely reaction. Defence is a normal reaction to attack. If we feel that a question threatens our self-esteem by pointing to something negative, we will automatically try to defend ourselves with justifications, blame shifting, or plain denial.

FACE THE TRUTH HOWEVER PAINFUL

To become self-aware we need the right mindset, and we need to be pro-active in our search for the truth, but we also need the courage to lower our guard and face up to painful truths which might be uncovered. Therefore we have to decide what we are going to do if this happens. If we know that our immediate reaction will be to move into denial, as I did with the Taylor Johnson Test, then we will be prepared to deal with it by taking a deep breath and fixing our eyes on the goal ahead. Incentives are an important part of life. We need them, especially when the going is tough. Occasionally my colleague and I have directed a 2/3-day teaching conference both at home and abroad. It is always a bit of a marathon, but we keep going by promising ourselves a few days off at the end. If we have been in the Southern States of America we plan a short break on a beach in Florida. The incentive gives us the energy to continue speaking and praying with people from early morning to late in the evening.

We need to set our sights on becoming a people of integrity. In more ways than one the truth will set us free.[8] The truth about Jesus gives us the incentive and courage to pursue the truth about ourselves. The truth about ourselves frees us from our blindness and cover-ups that makes change so difficult.

We will be doing nothing more than skirt over the following questions unless we are determined to face up to the truth, however painful, because our objective is to become more like Jesus.

Know Yourself Questionnaire

It might be helpful to jot the answers down in a notebook or journal. This should force you to think and pray about the questions. Ask God to guide you into the truth about yourself. As you answer the questions remind yourself that God is on your side and longs to see you grow and change and is not against you. If, in the process, you find yourself facing an uncomfortable fact about your past, or something about your present way of life that needs dealing with, ask

God to show you the right person with whom to chat it over and pray with.

Understanding My Past
- Write a paragraph describing your mother.
- Write a paragraph describing your father.
- What person in your childhood had the greatest influence upon you for good?
- What person in your childhood had the greatest influence upon you for evil?
- What was the happiest memory of your childhood?
- What was the unhappiest memory of your childhood?
- Is there an incident in your past you don't like to think about?
- Is there something in the past that you have never resolved?
- How could this be resolved now?
- What are the positive things in your life today which are the direct result of something which happened in the past?
- What are the negative things in your life today – attitudes, feelings, behaviour, which are the direct result of experiences in your childhood?
- Describe those experiences and why they had a negative effect upon you.
- What plans do you have to change these negative attitudes, feelings, and behaviour (if any)?
- Is there anything in the past you have done or said which you should not have done or said, and for which you have never repented and received God's forgiveness?
- Is there anyone who has hurt you in the past you have not yet forgiven? What do you plan to do about this?

Understanding My Present
- Who are the people in your life you feel closest to?
- Is there anyone you can trust with your deepest secrets?
- Are you accountable to someone in your work place?

- Are you accountable to someone in your private life?
- Do you enjoy your own company?
- If not why not?
- Do you make friends easily?
- Are your friendships long lasting?
- What are your major commitments?
- Do you enjoy those commitments? Or is there something else you would rather be doing?
- Do you have a great need to be accepted by others?
- What do you do to earn that acceptance?
- How do you react to rejection?
- Do you see yourself as a leader?
- Or are you more comfortable in a support role?
- Do you sometimes feel like a square peg in a round hole?
- Describe those situations?
- What situations make you feel secure?
- What makes you feel insecure?
- Do you believe that God loves you as an individual?
- Can you relate to God as a loving Father?
- If not what is preventing this?
- What are your strengths?
- What are your weaknesses?
- Do you communicate easily with others?
- Do your family or friends have complaints about you?
- What are they?
- What are the most common criticisms you receive?
- How do you react to them?
- Have you had any repetitive dreams?
- What problems in your life are inclined to happen again and again?
- Have you done a Personality Analysis Test?
- If so describe any weaknesses that appeared and what you have done to rectify them.

Looking towards the Future

- What goals do you have for your life?

- What plans have you made for the future?
- Do you worry about finances?
- How well do you communicate with your family members?
- Are you a good listener?
- Do you dole out lots of advice to those who are younger?
- What are you doing to keep fit?
- Do you act your age?
- Are you comfortable about growing older?
- What sort of things about the future make you anxious or depressed?
- What are you looking forward to?
- If your life were to end today would you have any regrets?
- If so what are they, and is there anything you can do about them now?
- When you die what will you be missed for?
- Do you believe that the best is yet to come both in life and in death?

This sort of questionnaire will help us know ourselves better and may show up some difficulties. It would be helpful after answering the questionnaire to categorise any problem areas you have detected.

BRIDGE THE GAPS

Developing the right mindset and actively examining our lives will help us in our quest to know ourselves better. However, we will stop at this point in our journey if we don't determine to do more than just notice our inconsistencies. We have to take notice and then put in some effort to close the gaps. Our integrity is quickly threatened when we are aware of the discrepancies but do nothing about them. We need to develop an allergy to gaps. I occasionally suffer a bad reaction to certain foods. When it first happened all I felt was slightly nauseated. It was so slight that I failed to take notice of it, until I realised that my torso was covered in a rash. Gradually I have learned to discern that first sign of nausea more promptly, which enables me to check my diet quickly. Those who truly desire to follow after holiness will develop a heightened sensitivity to gaps, however slight.

One of the inconsistencies that compromises our integrity most of all is the gap between what we believe and how we behave, or what we say and what we do. I have a friend whose whole life had been marked by a lack of punctuality, until one day she was addressing a meeting and speaking about the amazing fact of God's love and patience with us, and how we should value each other in the same way. As she spoke she felt a stab of acute discomfort. In her mind she heard the words: 'You hypocrite!' She suddenly realised that her tardiness was proof that she did not value people as she was telling others they must. Up until that moment she had suffered occasional discomfort when she was late for an appointment. But after that she developed an allergy to being late. She was quick to close the rift by finding ways that would help her become a punctual person. She knew she had to 'walk the talk'.

There is nothing wrong in having a gap between where we are and where we want to be as long as we are honest about it, and are working on bridging it. The loss of integrity comes when we haven't noticed the gulf, or have noticed it and do not attempt to work at it. I recently had lunch with a group of women who all desired to be part of the healing ministry team in their church. The only thing that seemed to be preventing them was their feelings of weakness and unworthiness. This was largely due to their respect and awe for a lady who sat at the table with us. She had been in the healing ministry for many years and was an experienced counsellor. They all felt unable to reach her high standard. I assured them that in the healing ministry there is never a point at which one feels worthy or sufficiently gifted, but that we all have to start somewhere.

I hoped the acknowledged expert would agree with me,

but she took no steps to fend off their adulation. I was surprised at the obvious gaps these ladies were prepared to live with. First there was the gap between being observers and becoming participators in the gifts of the Spirit, which the group seemed unable to bridge. Then the 'expert' had allowed an unreal division to spring up between herself and her friends. No one can afford to be put on a pedestal. If it happens then the responsibility for bridging the gap and climbing down belongs to the person to whom it has happened. The late John Wimber was a very gifted man but consistently encouraged others to get involved in ministry. 'Everyone gets to play,' was a favourite saying of his. Whenever anyone tried to put him on a pedestal he would respond, 'There is only one hero and that's Jesus.' And then he would add something like – 'I'm just a fat man trying to get to heaven.' Immediately he had put himself on the same level as everyone else.

The problem with gifting is that others often place such people 'six foot above contradiction'. Then gaps can easily appear between gifting and character. Gifting has nothing to do with character. In fact it is easy for a gifted person to rely on his talents and to let his character slip.

Miriam, Moses' sister, was a very gifted lady. She showed great initiative as a young girl when the Egyptian princess found her brother Moses in the bulrushes and she suggested their own mother as a wet nurse. She was also a leader and a prophetess. After Moses led the Children of Israel out of Egypt there was great rejoicing and at one point the prophetess, Miriam, took a tambourine in her hand and all the women followed her dancing and singing. But despite her gifting she harboured resentment against her brother Moses and his Cushite wife. The Lord was so displeased that he allowed her to become leprous. Only the prayers of Moses saved her. God is not as impressed as we are with gifting – it came from him in the first place. He is more interested in our humility and holiness.

We have to develop a sensitivity to gaps of this sort and do all that we can to bridge them. However, while working at this we should not miss the opportunity they may afford us to know ourselves better.

SEEK HEALING IF NEEDED

It is possible that Miriam's jealousy had a deeper cause. When we become aware of rifts in our lives we should always check in case they are a manifestation of something more, because if they are, they will continue to cause us problems until they are dealt with. Miriam had spent her life in slavery to the Egyptians. She had always been treated like a captive. Despite her experience of freedom perhaps she still carried captivity in her heart. When our past is not laid to rest we can drag it around with us like a ball and chain. We may long to grow and to change but we seem to make very little headway. Difficult feelings keep surfacing and these are then acted out in our behaviour.

One woman confided to me that she had recently been feeling very depressed and lacking in energy. When questioned about her present situation she said that her family, though living at home, were all very occupied with their own lives and she felt like their slave – there to wait on them when they needed something. She said she felt resentful and angry at the way she was being treated, but rather than say anything she had just become depressed. She kept repeating, 'I feel like a second class citizen.' As we met together the story of her life gradually came out. Like Miriam she had felt devalued as a child and had always seen herself as less important than her brother. She had never dealt with the resentment and bitterness that she had harboured as a result. Now it was being resurrected in the present and she was dealing with it in exactly the same way. Instead of standing up for herself she had become depressed and had retreated into her shell. By talking and praying with a second party this lady was able to do more than admit to her present discomfort. She was able to unravel her past, understand it better, and recognise how she had managed to drag it into the present. At the end of the time we spent together she knew herself far better than before.

It is up to us to take responsibility for our lives and to seek healing where it is needed. We can't expect God to operate on us without our knowledge, or co-operation. When we become pro-active and ask someone else to talk and pray with us, we are more likely to reach the truth about the past, about our reactions to it, and about our present behaviour. We come away with an understanding that will be the key to changing and growing.

BE ACCOUNTABLE

Perhaps we have received healing for the past and are well on the road to maturity, but none of us have arrived there yet. We have to be prepared to help one another on the journey. Only in extenuating circumstances is the Christian life meant to be lived alone. It has always been 'a group outing'. It must be possible for all of us to have another person or a group of people to whom we can be accountable.

I once heard Juan Carlos Ortiz accuse us of being like new potatoes instead of mashed ones. He said that most of the time we just bump up against one another and then go our separate ways. But Jesus wanted us to become one – mashed together. Friendship is a precious commodity and true friendship should provide the environment for accountability. 'We need others physically, emotionally, intellectually; we need them if we are to know anything, even ourselves.'[9] Within a good healthy relationship there should be challenge. Friends should hold up a mirror for us to see ourselves. Without challenge and confrontation there is unlikely to be any change. Richard Dortch, the man who went to prison for fraud over the Jimmy Bakker scandal, says that everyone needs a select group of people to whom they can be totally accountable. This group doesn't need to be

large or influential, they must simply care enough about you
to tell you what you need to hear.[10]

However, sometimes it seems harder to receive truth
about ourselves from our friends, than it is from someone
outside our immediate circle. My best friend has always
been my husband David. We are usually open and frank
with one another and although this has been painful at
times, it has also been very healthy. But sometimes those
closest may not seem as objective as someone further away.
Occasionally, even though it may appear to be a bit of a
cop-out, seeing a relative stranger may be a good option.

Several years ago I decided to make a silent retreat at a
nearby convent. I was allotted one of the Nuns to oversee
my time. The idea was that I saw her first thing in the morning and she suggested a pattern for the day. The hour I spent
with this lady was a revelation. She was a very experienced
spiritual director and knew exactly what sort of questions to
ask me. I found the time I spent with her, and then the time
spent in praying and reading at her direction an eye-opener!
I came away from that time with insights about myself I
would never have arrived at on my own, or with close
friends.

Spiritual direction on a regular basis is not possible for
all of us. There are not enough Christians trained in this discipline to go around. But an occasional retreat should be a
possibility for most of us. This may be a solitary one or a
group retreat. About ten years ago my colleague, Prue
Bedwell, and I decided that if people were given the opportunity to spend a few days examining their lives and meeting with God in the company of other like-minded people,
significant change could be achieved. So three times a year
for the past ten years we have been taking about 25–28 people away for a weekend's retreat and we have been amazed
by the letters we have received later telling of significant
changes that have occurred as a result. These times have
encouraged me almost more than anything else I have been

involved in.

There is much we can do to help ourselves in our pursuit of self-awareness. However we must bear in mind that 'we' are not the objective. Our goal must be constantly kept in view otherwise we will end up in a downward spiral of unhealthy introspection. The objective always has to be to become more like Jesus.

Chapter Ten

THE BLESSINGS OF INTEGRITY

'While truth is freeing it is far from free: truth asks everything in our lives that contradicts it.'[1]

When I was a child my father had a safe kept under the stairs in the hall. As far as I knew he never touched the money inside. My mother, who was the last of the big spenders and went shopping for pure enjoyment, longed to get her hands on it. But however much she moaned at Dad and accused him of letting it go mouldy, the money continued to lie idle. I never saw him open the safe and often wondered if he had lost the key. I imagined stacks of money all turning gradually greener with mould. Qualities such as authenticity, honesty and credibility are far more valuable than my Dad's money, but they may never be achieved without the key of self-awareness.

Self-knowledge guards us from deceiving ourselves in the myriad, clever ways we sometimes do. Self-awareness, therefore, is not our goal. It is just the key to living a life of integrity, which is the sort of life Jesus led. He was known as a man of 'integrity' because he taught the way of God in accordance with the truth without being swayed by what others thought.[2] When used of Jesus the word integrity simply means 'truth'. If we desire to become more like Jesus then we will strive for truth. In the Bible the word 'integrity' usually comes from the Hebrew word *tom* or *tamam* which means complete, perfect, upright, innocent. And sometimes words like 'faithful' and 'trustworthy' in the King James Version, are replaced in the New International Version with 'integrity'. Becoming like Jesus means developing all the attributes which make up integrity. It is a high calling – a wonderful goal to aspire to. Such a goal is not an easy option and will call for energy and determination.

DISCOMFORT

Because avoidance of truth is often used to escape discomfort, then it stands to reason that facing the truth will sometimes be uncomfortable, and that occasionally it will take courage for us to face reality. I remember a young man confessing that he had once made a mistake and cheated on his wife. He asked me what I thought he should do about it. It had happened several years previously and he had rationalised that what his wife didn't know about wouldn't hurt her. Then he became a Christian and his conscience began to prick him. It was painful for him to face the truth that what he had done was wrong, not just a mistake. He eventually found the courage and an appropriate time to confess his infidelity to his wife and together they worked through the difficult feelings. In the end their marriage was stronger, but it was not easy for either of them. It was a hard step but the right one (given the right moment) towards the goal of integrity.

One of our greatest needs is to be accepted and our greatest fear is rejection. Therefore to have to tell someone an unpalatable truth is difficult. I once had to tell a lady that she was not able to serve on the ministry team that I was leading. She was a very needy person and had some rather weird and distracting mannerisms. I knew she would feel rejected, and I knew she wouldn't like me for turning her down, consequently I had to grit my teeth before I found the courage to confront her. An honest confrontation might not, at first, be considered an act of integrity, but in the long run it generates more trust than taking the course of least

resistance, which would be to belittle and criticise, or partici-
pate in gossip about another behind his/her back.[3] But if it's
hard to face someone else with unpalatable truth, perhaps it
is even harder to be faced with distasteful truth about oneself. To wake up to the fact that one has an irritating habit,
or a less than loving attitude is painful. One tends to feel
rejected and want to defend oneself. But if truth is the goal,
then part of achieving the goal will be to face the discomfort
of hearing what we would rather not hear.

A life dedicated to truth is not easy. 'It means a continuous and never-ending process of self-monitoring to assure
that our communications – not only the words that we say
but also the way we say them – invariably reflect as accurate-
ly as humanly possible the truth or reality as we know it.'[4]
Some people would rather opt for a life of shadows and darkness rather than live in the sunlight where nothing can be hidden. They choose never to examine themselves, notice their
inconsistencies or make themselves accountable to others. It
takes effort to 'notice'. It demands attention to detail and it
demands that when we do notice something skewed in our
life that we make some effort to change it. Jesus himself said
that 'men loved darkness instead of light because their deeds
were evil.'[5]

CHALLENGE

'A life of total dedication to the truth also means a life of
willingness to be personally challenged.'[6] In the past I have
occasionally agreed to see families who have found themselves in difficulties. Sometimes an objective outsider can
see the blockage better than those within the system. Every
time I have had this opportunity I have been amazed at the
family's courage. They are opening their lives to scrutiny,
analysis and possible criticism. I remember one father sitting
there open-mouthed on hearing his son's frank observations
about the way their family worked – or in this case wasn't
working. He was obviously moved and very challenged by

his son's words. It was interesting to see how the mother was less able to absorb the criticism than the father. She immediately came to her own defence and was less open to the challenge than her husband had been.

Challenge can either be welcomed or ignored. If we are seriously involved in trying to change and become like Jesus, then it will be welcomed. It is in these circumstances that a previously determined mindset will assist us. It will guarantee a willingness to accept personal challenge with a degree of excitement. It's as if we are on a journey of discovery that we have already realised might not be all comfort and ease. But the destination beckons us on. When we lived in South America we would take the family on camping holidays. Because there were no such things as organised camping sites, we often could not plan where we would actually camp. Instead we would set off in the general direction of a lake or river which looked interesting on the map. It was always exciting to imagine the Utopia we might find. Certainly over the years we found some very beautiful places, but we also had a few uncomfortable experiences. We once skidded on a dirt track road and careered off the road near the Argentine border, at quite a high altitude. We tried to dig ourselves out but to no avail. The road was lonely and the traffic very sparse. A truck did eventually come to our rescue, but it meant that we had to make camp rather late. The height meant that the temperature dropped significantly during the night, so we all squeezed into one small tent and cuddled up together fully dressed. During those adventurous holidays we faced some discomfort and hard challenges, but saw some amazing scenery and met some wonderful people, all of which we would have missed had we settled for comfort and ease.

Challenge is received but it may also be given. If we value the truth then occasionally we may be called upon to challenge other people's lies. The Bible calls it provoking one another to good works.[7] *Hello* magazine once published an interview with Erin Brockovich, whose story was made into a film. It tells how Erin locked horns and challenged the activities of a corrupt public utility which were slowly poisoning a whole community. She came from a family who placed a high value on honesty. When she was 15 she had lied to her father about a trip to Chicago. When her father found out she was punished. The next day he wrote her a letter saying that he realised that their confrontation the night before had torn her up as it had him. 'But if you, your brothers and sister, your mother and I cannot freely and honestly communicate with each other, then we have lost everything.' He ended the letter by telling her that he and her mother loved her very much and wanted her to develop into an admired, honest and respected woman. 'Together we can be assured it will be accomplished.'[8] That experience and her family's emphasis on truthfulness had an influence on Erin which gave her moral calibre and the courage to confront, and overcome the 'giant'.

Living a life of integrity is not easy, but it is eminently worthwhile.

CLEAR SIGHT

Jesus warns us not to judge others before we have first judged ourselves. If we fail to sort out our own lives how can we possibly have the clarity and ability to help someone else with their lives. He makes the point by asking a ridiculous question. 'Why do you look at the speck of sawdust in your brother's eye and pay no attention to the plank in your own eye? How can you say to your brother, "Let me take the speck out of your eye," when all the time there is a plank in your own eye? You hypocrite, first take the plank out of your own eye, and then you will see clearly to remove the speck from your brother's eye.'[9]

The process of self-examination, of dawning awareness of our frailties and faults and the subsequent endeavour to put right what is wrong, clarifies our vision. The benefits of being an authentic, credible and honest person are immeasurable. The best of which must be the blessing accorded to those of pure heart – they shall have a clear vision of God. 'Blessed are the pure in heart for they will see God.'[10] Isn't that what we all long for?

Not only will we have a more perfect vision of God, but we will be in a position to discern and help others who want to grow and change. After a tragic life of rejection and abuse a young woman who had undergone several years of counselling, decided to do a counselling course herself. She excelled at it because she understood the way human beings tick. She knew what sort of strategies those hurt by the world resort to and how they try and minimise, even escape, suffering and pain. She understood the games people play to avoid the truth, and she knew that facing the pain would lead to freedom. Her wisdom didn't come solely from the counselling course. Mostly it came out of her own experience as she learned the difficult task of walking the road towards wholeness, and worked at removing the 'plank' in her own eye.

Another advantage of knowing oneself well is that it heightens one's ability to sense hype and hypocrisy of any kind. Perhaps this is because someone who has recognised the potential within themselves for deceit and sham is quick to spot those who have fallen into the trap, and are yet unaware of it.

GUIDANCE

'The integrity of the upright guides them.'[11] At different times in our life we all need guidance. How often have I sighed, and heard others groaning because finding the will of God is so difficult. What makes it easier is self-awareness. A person who has taken the trouble to examine himself and has cleared away inner confusion and hurt which might be contaminating his motives, is freer to hear God's voice than a person who lives in ignorance of his inner drives and unmet needs. A young wife asked her husband if he would go with her to see a marriage guidance counsellor because she thought they could do with some help in communicating. The man agreed to go for the first interview but after that said he wasn't prepared to go to any more, because he wasn't going to mess around navel gazing! Sadly that sort of attitude is very common, but it misses the point. A better understanding of the way he functioned as a person might have helped him get a handle on why his marriage wasn't working out very well. Living in ignorance is like choosing to stumble around in the dark, when one has the option of turning on the light and seeing where one is going.

Whenever someone asks me to pray with them for guidance they nearly always ask me how they can tell if this is what God wants them to do or is it just something they want for themselves. The fact is our motives influence what we are doing all the time. We are never free of them, nor would we wish to be. 'A world without motives would be a world without excitement, enthusiasm and fulfilment; without hopes, dreams and ambitions.'[12] The key to getting guidance right is to know ourselves well enough to know what motivates us. Then we are in a position to discern between what is purely a need for significance or security on our part, and God's call on our lives, though these needs are very pressing ones and, to a degree, will always play a part in the decisions we make. However, being honest, having mixed motives is the sad condition of the human heart. It's not lack of integrity to admit that one has not yet arrived at one's desired destination. It's wrong when we pretend that we have. To know God's guidance we must know the state of our own heart and its true motives.

FAMILY BLESSING

'The just man walketh in his integrity: his children are blessed after him.'[13] The formative years of children's lives are the years they spend in their family home – the years between nought and eighteen. During that time they are developing physically, mentally, socially, emotionally and spiritually. Though not totally mature by eighteen, nevertheless, they will never again experience a time of such rapid growth. After the age of eighteen the graph slows down considerably though it never ends completely. Educationalists tell us that a child acquires knowledge best through seeing and hearing. Therefore it is vital that a parent models honesty, trustworthiness, and faithfulness in front of the child as well as talks about it. Integrity is caught rather than taught.

A mother and father may be keen that their children grow up to be morally upright citizens and so insist on certain standards. However, those demands will go in one ear and out of the other if the lives of their parents do not match their words. For example a father may demand honesty from his children and punish them if they lie, but then he is overheard by the children telling his wife how he stayed with a friend on a recent business trip instead of a hotel, and adds with a laugh, 'But I'll jolly well charge them [meaning his firm] for the hotel.' The children are learning that adults are happy to lie when it suits them. Perhaps a mother demands punctuality at meals from the children, but is consistently late picking them up from school. Or even worse children may be punished for cheating, and then one of their parents is discovered cheating on the other by committing adultery.

These inconsistencies damage a child's trust and the very foundations of their integrity. What especially blesses a child is to see the parent careful about keeping promises, and what damages the relationship is when promises are treated lightly. Stephen Covey likens it to making bank deposits or withdrawals. 'Keeping a commitment or a promise is a major deposit; breaking one is a major withdrawal.' He explained that to make a promise that's important to someone and then not to come through with it is a massive withdrawal. He said that as a parent he always tried never to make a promise that he didn't keep, and therefore he made them very carefully and sparingly. However, if despite his best efforts, he was forced to break it he would explain the situation very carefully to the person involved and asked to be released from the promise. Or if he did something wrong then he would apologise. 'When we make withdrawals from the Emotional Bank Account we need to apologise and we need to do it sincerely. Great deposits come in the sincere words: "I was wrong." "That was unkind." "I showed you no respect."' These are the attitudes and actions of a person with integrity, and when they are demonstrated they bless our children.[14]

A child whose parents try to be scrupulously honest in all their doings, and are openly repentant if something happens to compromise that standard, is being handed a priceless gift. It may only be later that he recognises the solid foundation of trust and security on which his life has been built. To have been brought up in a home where one can relax in the knowledge that whatever the parent says it will be the truth to the best of his or her knowledge, and that human failure and frailty will be openly acknowledged, is an incalculable blessing. So often I have heard a person comment with pride about his dad's integrity. Just the other day I heard a man talking about his father and laughing about his foibles, but then added proudly, 'but he was such a man of integrity.'

Dr Laura Schlessinger tells the story of a man called Harvey. He had filled his truck with fuel and after he had paid realised he had been given an extra $5 change. He immediately went back to the cashier and returned the extra money. The cashier thanked him and told him that this had only happened once before and that was about twenty years previously. The cashier remembered that the customer had been a little older than Harvey but his vehicle was a van and had the same signs on the side as had Harvey's. Harvey realised that honest customer had been his father. He com-

mented, 'I was very fortunate to be able to work side by side
with my father for many years. This is but one of the lessons
I learned from him by example.'[15]

PEACE AND PROTECTION

'The man of integrity walks securely.'[16] He has no fear of
authority because he has not broken the law. His heart does
not condemn him because he is innocent of wrong doing.
So he walks at peace with himself and the world. Since the
September 11th attacks in New York there has been some
suggestion that for the safety of society it would be good for
everyone to carry an identity card. Some people are anxious
that such a step would infringe our civil liberties. When we
lived in South America we all carried identity cards, as we
did during the Second World War, and thought nothing of
it. Only if we had something to hide would we have had
cause to fear.

Stephen Covey suggests that intrinsic security comes
from within and not from what other people think of us or
how they treat us. Nor does it come from our circumstances
or our position, but 'it comes from accurate paradigms and
correct principles deep in our own mind and heart. It comes
from inside-out congruence, from living a life of integrity in
which our daily habits reflect our deepest values.' He goes
on to say that he believes that a life of integrity is the most
fundamental source of personal worth and that peace of
mind comes when one's life is in harmony with true principles and values and in no other way.[17]

However people do fall short often, both of their own
standards and those of God. So are we doomed to a life of
condemnation? My favourite chapter in the Bible is in
Romans where Paul says that there is no condemnation for
those who are in Christ Jesus.[18] Years ago I read the story of
a little boy who had been caught being naughty and had
been punished by his father. He was very upset, not just
because he had been found out, but also because he felt so

guilty for what he had done and didn't know how to put it right. His father took him into his study, picked up a piece of paper and drew a circle. Around the circle he marked a number of doors and called them names like, deceit, teasing, disobedience, lying, rudeness, cheating etc. Then he told his son that when he found himself outside the safety of the circle the way back was always through the same door as the one by which he had left. He needed to confess that particular sin and ask forgiveness for it and where possible make restitution to get back in. As soon as the little boy did this he was at peace. He was back 'in Christ' again – the safe place where there is no condemnation.

A life of integrity means peace from a guilty conscience and also peace from 'the rats in the cupboard'. Our open-plan lifestyle means that whatever rats were once there have all been expelled. There is now no hidden agenda, no untold secrets, no suppressed traumas left to jump out and frighten us. We don't have to be on our guard any more. We are free to discuss any subject. Our life history can be shared if it is deemed appropriate. This does not mean that we won't ever feel depressed or frightened again, but that we will know why. Understanding why we feel as we do largely takes the fear out of painful feelings. The feeling may be negative, but understanding it makes it a legitimate and an acceptable part of our present experience. Our mental health is threatened the moment we begin to partition off, suppress, or avoid painful truth. In fact Scott Peck says that mental health is an ongoing process of dedication to reality at all costs.[19]

I remember once asking a young girl I knew if she would come to a meeting with me and give her testimony. She had a history of childhood rejection and abuse and for many people such painful memories are very hard to talk about. But her response was that if it would be helpful for other people to hear her story she would be willing to tell it. She stood up that evening, visibly moved as she spoke, but com-

pletely able to re-visit the places in her life that had once
been so painful that she had tried to bury them and pretend
they didn't exist. Now 'the rats in the cupboard' had been
cleaned out. It was such an obvious demonstration of mental and emotional health.

Another threat to our peace of mind is when we attempt
to please too many people. The root meaning of the word
integrity is completeness. It means the heart is intact and
not divided. We are not trying to serve two masters, which
Jesus says is impossible.[20] Integrity means that whatever the
cost we are putting God's kingdom and his righteousness
first in our lives. Once something comes between us and
that goal we lose our integrity and our peace of mind. The
church leader who tries to please every member of the
church ends up sitting on the fence, which is a very uncomfortable perch and the peace he so desires eludes him.
Deciding to please God means to risk losing popularity with
some, but he keeps his peace of mind in the knowledge that,
to the best of his ability, he is serving God.

We are all impacted and influenced by the example of
others. It could have been someone in a book, a film, or a
personal meeting. More than ever today young people are
looking for leaders, men and women of integrity, that they
admire and whose example they can follow. In these days of
such uncertainty many are looking for hope, direction and
spiritual help. The post-modern laxity with truth and smor-
gasbord of beliefs will help no one. It is an amazing opportunity for the church. But unless we have leaders of integrity we will fail in the task.

Chapter Eleven

INTEGRITY AND LEADERSHIP

'Integrity is not what we do as much as who we are.'[1]

In the film *Scent of a Woman*, Al Pacino plays the part of a blind army veteran whose friend is a young boy called Charlie, played by Chris O'Donnell. Charlie attends a very prestigious private school in Boston, where he has an assisted place. He finds himself in serious trouble because he refuses to squeal on some colleagues whom he witnessed playing a trick on the headmaster. The headmaster tries to get the information out of Charlie by bribing him with a place at Harvard if he tells on his mates. By refusing Charlie knows that he has ruined his future prospects. At the end of the film the headmaster gathers the whole school and publicly condemns Charlie's refusal to co-operate with the authorities. There is no one to speak up for Charlie until at the last moment Frank, his blind friend, walks into the Great Hall, strides to the platform and makes a heart-rending speech in defence of his friend. He challenges the school, which he describes as 'the cradle of leadership', 'the makers of men', to think what kind of leaders they were making there. He commends Charlie because he wouldn't sell anybody out to buy his future. 'That's called integrity. That's called conscience. That's the stuff leaders should be made of.' When Frank sits down the school rises to its feet cheering and the viewer is left mouthing a silent, but heartfelt, 'Yes'.[2] Because deep down we all believe that leadership and integrity should go hand in hand.

Nelson Mandela was a brilliant statesman and a leader of outstanding charisma. He was described as a typical postmodernist leader who was the master of imagery and performance. Despite all this he possessed a moral authority and concern for the truth with which few could compete. He remained a master of symbolic images, but in the end it was his essential integrity more than his superhuman myth which gave his story its appeal across the world.[3] His life proves that it is possible for leaders to be men of integrity.

Leaders are people who have influence over others and certain qualities are required of them. In this chapter I am confining myself to the subject of church leadership; however the same principles apply also in the home, office, factory or school. A leader may be male or female, may be leading ten, fifty, a hundred or a thousand people. Though I mostly refer to the leader as 'he' it is not because I am sexist but simply because trying to be politically correct and addressing them both at the same time seems so clumsy and difficult in the text. I ask that the ladies forgive me and believe that I have them in mind just as much as their male counterparts. In fact I have met some very good women in leadership and my personal observation has been that they tend to be more real and honest about themselves than many men.

Surveys conducted over ten years by James Kouzes and Barry Posner, leadership experts, all came up with the same top qualities required of a leader. The number one attribute was honesty. When more than fifteen hundred managers were questioned they provided 225 values, characteristics, and attitudes that they believed crucial to leadership. A panel of researchers analysed the findings and once again integrity came top of the list.[4] John Maxwell, who is not only a successful leader himself, but also writes and lectures extensively on the subject calls integrity the most important ingredient of leadership. He says that it is a vanishing commodity today. 'Personal standards are crumbling in a world that has taken to hot pursuit of personal pleasure and shortcuts to success.'[5]

WHY IS INTEGRITY SUCH AN IMPORTANT INGREDIENT FOR A LEADER?

Integrity is an important quality in the life of every Christian, but for a leader it is essential. The start of the twenty-first century will be remembered for its hype, spin, stretching the truth and making 'idols' out of footballers, pop stars and models. Even in the Christian church we are dazzled by gifted men and women and often elevate their gifting above their character. We have a tendency to be superficial in our judgements and fail to look beneath the surface at the person's inner life. We often ask searching questions about his gifts, but gloss over his relationship with God and whether he is patient with his children and kind to his wife. However, disillusionment soon sets in when a leader fails to meet the godly standards we unconsciously long to see in those who are there to guide us.

Integrity Engenders Trust

The more integrity a leader shows the more trust he is given. Every time he does what he says he is going to do he makes a deposit in his trust account. Every time he practises what he preaches he makes a deposit. Every time he shows kindness to insignificant people, or notices seemingly unimportant tasks that people are doing and makes a point of thanking them, he makes a deposit. Dwight Eisenhower said that in order to be a leader a man must have followers. And to have followers, a man must have their confidence.[6] A leader makes withdrawals from his trust account and destroys the confidence of his followers whenever:

- He breaks a promise
- Doesn't live the life he talks about
- Gives a false prophecy
- Launches the church into a costly but useless project
- Fails to give credit where credit is due
- Is not totally honest with people
- Shows little interest in his people's lives
- Is invisible as a leader
- Is the cause of scandal
- Betrays a confidence
- Doesn't apologise for his mistakes.

When these things happen trust is eroded, and though he may still be the leader in name, he will risk losing some followers and diminish the trust of others.

When the ex-president, Bill Clinton was found to have lied over his smutty little affair with Monica Lewinsky the question must have crossed the public's mind as to whether he could be trusted to tell the truth about vital and important public matters of State. Certainly in God's kingdom only those who have shown themselves faithful in little will be given greater responsibility, because they have proved themselves trustworthy.[7]

Integrity aids Discernment

To be a good leader one has to have wisdom and discernment. There will be many instances in a leader's life when he will be called upon to make important decisions, or to discern what direction the Lord is leading the church. When Solomon became king he could have asked God for anything he liked – riches, fame, popularity or the death of his enemies. In fact all he asked for was discernment. 'So give your servant a discerning heart to govern your people and to distinguish between right and wrong.' God was so delighted that he granted this request as well as all the other things he had not asked for.[8] An example of the outworking of this prayer was seen when two prostitutes came to him with their babies, one dead and one alive. Both claimed that the living one was theirs. Solomon asked for a sword and gave the order that the living child should be cut in half, and each woman given half a baby. 'The woman whose son was alive was filled with compassion for her son and pleaded with the king, "Please, my lord give her the living baby! Don't kill him." . . . When all Israel heard the verdict the king had given, they held the king in awe, because they saw that he had wisdom from God to administer justice.'[9]

It is an interesting fact that God commanded Aaron, who was the High Priest, to carry the Urim and Thummim in his breastplate when he went in before the Lord. Though we have little information as to what these stones were or how they were used exactly, their purpose was to help the High Priest make decisions for the children of Israel. The word 'Urim' meant light and the word 'Thummim' perfection and comes from the root word *tom* which could be translated integrity.[10] Aaron needed truth and integrity when he had to make judgements or decisions for the children of Israel.

Integrity is vitally important for the discerning process. When a leader lacks integrity his judgement will be affected. It is important that he is able to lay aside his own desires and put those for whom he is responsible first. One of the words the *Oxford Dictionary* uses to define integrity is 'wholeness'. A person who, for whatever reason, has unhealed hurts, unfinished business, or cordoned off areas in his life will sometimes make decisions which may be influenced by the hidden issues in his life which have been pushed out of sight. For example a leader who has known serious rejection as a child will have a tendency to be driven by a gnawing need to be accepted. Providing this inner need is acknowledged by him and he is actively working at it, he will be able to stand back and be objective in his judgements. But if this is a buried issue that he cannot face, then unconsciously his decisions are in danger of being influenced by his fear of rejection. Or a leader who is under strain and has begun to drink too much alcohol in order to cope, but has placed his addiction in a secret area of his life, he may easily resort to lies to hide his actions from others. How can he make unbiased, clear decisions under those circumstances?

Integrity in a Leader sets an Example

'Eighty-nine percent of what people learn comes through visual stimulation, ten percent through audible stimulation, and one percent through other senses. So it makes sense that the more followers see and hear their leader being consistent in word and action, the greater their consistency and loyalty. . . What people need is not a motto to say, but a model to see.'[11]

When David and I came to St Andrew's Church, Chorleywood, we found a very loving church. It was remarkable the care that radiated into the community from the believers there. We soon realised that love had been a very important and visible element in the previous leader's style. The people had just followed his example. A leader has to 'understand that people only *listen* to preaching; they *emulate* behaviour.'[12]

Integrity that is modelled by the leader, not just talked about, will be embraced joyfully by his followers. A person of integrity is complete. He is integrated. He is the sort of person that takes his own advice, and practises what he preaches. He is the sort of person who is the same in public as in private. Not like the young leader I heard of the other day who was careful with his language when he was in a religious gathering but when he went down to the pub with his mates his language was embarrassing. When the fruits of the Spirit are manifest in a leader's life it sets the tone for everything else that happens in the church. But they have to be integrated into his whole life, so that all the time, both in public and private he is a godly person.

WHAT THREATENS A LEADER'S INTEGRITY?

Another dictionary definition of integrity is 'soundness'. A leader must be true through and through. He cannot afford to be two-faced.

Unreality or Insincerity

So many leaders have a public persona, which they wear for the up-front occasion, and they have a private one which they wear at home. 'Image is what people think we are. Integrity is what we really are.'[13] Some leaders consciously develop an image with which to impress others. Such people keep a distance between themselves and their people and because few people ever see them in relaxed mode the image is all they know. For a while it is enough to be dazzled by the apparent importance, gifting, and authority of the leader, but after a while the unreality begins to show and people become dissatisfied. People want to know their leader. They know they can't all have a close relationship but they want to know what sort of person he or she really is. And they want reality not some pseudo figure.

I remember once being asked how I was by the leader of a church. I started to tell him, thinking he was interested, when I realised his attention had wandered and he was looking around. As I hesitated, not knowing whether to continue or not, he quickly turned back to me and flashed me a sympathetic smile. So I started again, but I soon realised that asking me how I was did not mean he wanted to hear. Concern was just one of those things a leader was meant to have. I felt like offering to help him with his 'listening skills'. But even learning to do the job better is not necessarily the real thing.

John Maxwell says that leaders who are sincere don't have to advertise the fact. It's visible in everything they do. It soon becomes common knowledge to everyone. In the same way insincerity cannot be hidden, disguised, or covered up, no matter how competent a man may otherwise be.

He goes on to suggest that the only way to keep the esteem and goodwill of the people you work with is to deserve it. 'No one can fool all of the people all of the time. Each of us, eventually, is recognised for exactly what we are – not what we try to appear to be.'[14]

Being a Square Peg in a Round Hole

One of the problems facing the church today is not recognising a person's gifting. Whenever people are put in a job for which they are not suited they quickly begin to feel the strain. My husband once worked under a very godly man who did not have the gifting for the very complex situation he was asked to lead. Consequently he became very stressed, acted out of character and made some wrong decisions. Soon those he was trying to lead became disillusioned and angry. In the body of Christ there are apostles, prophets, evangelists, pastors and teachers. The leader's job is to see that those five areas are adequately covered, but not necessarily by him.

Max DePree says that understanding and accepting diversity enables us to see that each of us is needed. It also enables us to begin to think about being abandoned to the strengths of others; of admitting that we cannot know or do everything.[15] We all need to be involved in the ministry we are most fitted for and not be straining to do those things for which we have no gifting. If we move out of our gifting the stress will soon begin to show.

For a short while, during our early years in Chile, my husband had to be both administrator and treasurer for the mission in our region. Not having the gifting for this job meant that he felt unhappy and unfulfilled. It was interesting to see the change when a young woman came to our area with office skills and took the job over. She was fulfilled, and he was happy. So often in the church we find men and women in the wrong roles. They are square pegs in round holes, and their integrity is threatened, because they are con-

stantly being asked to do things for which they are not suited. Soon the stress begins to show and they start acting out
of character and lose their integrity.

INSECURITY

John Maxwell says that to be a great developer of people,
which every leader should be, you must be personally
secure, because taking your people to the height of their
potential may mean they will pass you by.[16] Insecurity
threatens integrity, because it influences a person's decisions. A secure leader will make every effort to assemble a
high-calibre staff with the potential for future leadership.
An insecure one will usually have people around him of
inferior gifting who will be no challenge to his position or
influence.

Insecurity is a stumbling block for a leader. Everyone
will make mistakes but insecure people find it very hard to
climb off their pedestal long enough to apologise sincerely.
It makes them feel too vulnerable. Instead of apologising for
mistakes an insecure leader tends to make excuses for them,
blame other people, minimise or rationalise them away.
Such a person's integrity is threatened because he is unable
to face the truth. A young man once came to see us because
he had been forced to resign from two different churches.
He blamed his predicament on the unkind treatment he had
received from other staff members. In fact he had frequently become very angry and had been challenged about his bad
temper, but he resented the criticism and was unable to face
up to his inappropriate behaviour. He never apologised and
as a result his position became untenable and he had to
resign. When we saw him he was without a position, but
was still blaming everyone else for his predicament.

Insecurity jeopardises a leader's integrity, because
unconsciously he will protect himself from it by avoiding
every situation that threatens his security. Committee meetings may be cut short or cancelled, confrontation will be

avoided, other people's opinions will probably never be asked, no public debate is ever likely to take place, and so his decisions will pass unchallenged. Gradually the trust and confidence of the members dwindle, until finally the leader finds himself in a very isolated and lonely place.

Immorality

Perhaps it should go without saying that any hint of immorality threatens a leader's integrity. Again, no one is without sin. We all fall short of God's standards. But human frailty is one thing, deliberate sin is another. A leader who is secretly practising immorality has already lost his integrity, though others don't yet know it. The inconsistency is bound to spill over and gradually affect the rest of his life. Lies will be told to cover up sin, and lies beget lies. The hidden rot has set in and the tree will soon fall. When the sin is eventually uncovered, as it will be, those closest will pay the price with a painful sense of betrayal and disillusionment.

Followers want a leader they can admire and be proud of. Parents want figures in the sports and entertainment world for their children to emulate. When public figures are not just gifted but show integrity it is a real bonus. In William Bennett's book *The Death of Outrage*, he bemoans the fact that there was little public outrage about Bill Clinton's misconduct. He points out that with the use of diversion, half-truth, equivocation, and sophistry the president and his advisors built a defensive wall which remained unbreached. He stresses that all of us, but especially the young, need around us individuals who possess a certain nobility, a largeness of soul, and qualities of human excellence worth imitating and striving for. He named General Colin Powell as such a man. 'The extraordinary political appeal of General Colin Powell is rooted in his rock-solid character, his wartime valor, his faithfulness as a husband and father. He is the type of man that mothers can point to and say to their children, "Here is a man who fought for his country, honors his wife, loves his family. Be like that man."'17 Immorality doesn't just threaten, it destroys a leader's integrity, and without it he is a hollow shell. There is nothing left to emulate.

If these things threaten, what will strengthen a leader's integrity?

DEVELOPING INTEGRITY

If a person feels called to a leadership role, however small, it is worth spending a few moments addressing the subject of his or her own personal integrity. What does it look like? Do I have it? What sort of things would threaten it? How can I increase it?

Self-Awareness

The key to successful leadership is 'self-awareness'. Kouzes and Posner state that today's leaders should seek self-knowledge if they mean to establish and enhance their credibility . . . 'Your capacity to win the personal credibility jackpot – to align words and deeds – depends on how well you know yourself.'18 It is paramount for a leader to know his strengths and his weaknesses. To know where his particular gifts lie and where he needs to find someone else with different skills to fill the gaps. He needs to know his areas of vulnerability and insecurity, if any. All of us are in the process of maturing. None of us has yet arrived. Most of us have areas of our lives we still struggle with. But a leader, more than most, needs to know what areas those are, understand how they affect him, and particularly be aware of what situations are likely to trigger those difficult feelings. If he doesn't know himself he will sometimes find himself unconsciously acting in ways which baffle him and those around him.

We all need occasional time out to examine our lives and ask ourselves some pertinent questions, but a leader most of all. Questions such as:

- Am I overly concerned with my image and what people think of me?
- What situations make me anxious?
- What are my strengths?
- What are my gifts?
- What are my weaknesses and what am I doing to overcome them?
- Do I feel threatened by people's questions or do I welcome them?
- How do I react to criticism?
- How well do I handle confrontation?
- Do I feel threatened by other people's gifting?
- Do I value people?
- What sort of model am I for others to follow?
- Do I give others credit for their contribution to the life of the church and the work of God's kingdom?
- Am I an encouraging leader?
- Do I fear God?

The last question is the most important. A person who seeks to be a good leader should ask himself if he really fears God. I believe this is the thousand dollar question. Some sections of the Christian church have majored more on the immanence of God than on his transcendence. In other words they have enjoyed intimacy with God, which has been a wonderful discovery, but the danger then is that we forget that our God is a consuming fire – an awesome power who is totally other – a God who requires us to be holy as he is holy. The fear, or awe, of God is very salutary. It encourages us to examine our lives carefully, take note of the places where we are falling short, repent and amend our ways.

Now and again a leader should challenge himself. If he is brave enough he might even ask a close friend to go through the above questions with him.

Healing and Growth

Integrity means that a leader practises what he preaches. If he believes and teaches that Jesus longs for, and helps us, to become mature, whole and holy, then he has to be co-operating with the Holy Spirit himself in that process. He has to be prepared to seek inner healing wherever and whenever it is needed. This doesn't mean to say that he has to confess to his congregation his personal struggles and areas of weakness. That can often be counter-productive. But they just need to know that he is in a process as much as they are and is working at his weaknesses, just as he encourages them to. Occasionally it is helpful to use a personal illustration provided it is not used to manipulate people for sympathy or create an impression of humility. An example is only useful in so far as it encourages or helps others in their struggles.

Many leaders find themselves constantly ministering to others and rarely in a position to receive it themselves. It is vital that now and again they seek places where they can be on the receiving end of ministry in a secure environment. About fifteen years ago a retired clergyman and his wife moved into the village and offered to run leaders' retreats based in the parish. The men and women who came were billeted out on members of the church. Recently one of the host team died and there was a memorial service for him. A Finnish pastor flew over especially to attend the service. He had attended one of those retreats and had stayed with the deceased and his wife and they had ministered to him over the ten days he was with them. His testimony was that he had received a major healing which had changed his life and his ministry.

Admit to Mistakes and Apologise for them

When Kouzes and Posner asked people to list what behaviours best defined an honest person, 'admitting mistakes,' was mentioned second only to, 'telling the truth.'[19] As we have said, behind the inability to admit mistakes, and apologise for them, lies a deep-rooted insecurity. However, we are not healed of past hurts overnight. It takes time to grow into a place of security, but learning to admit to mistakes can start immediately. It is hard and painful to be wrong, whoever we are – especially when holding public office. But a pre-determined mindset will strengthen a leader to take the humble route and admit error. Once he realises its importance and determines to make it a discipline of life it will become gradually easier.

The following example is a poor illustration, but might help to make the point. When our children were small David and I would often have minor disagreements when we were travelling. I would attempt to read the map and give directions and David would put in his pennyworth while driving. If we got lost whose fault was it? I would blame him for interfering and he would blame me for mis-leading him. One day we were on a journey to Wales. The four girls were in the back and I was in the front with the map on my lap. I ordered a right turn, which David reluctantly took and then when we were thoroughly lost I realised I had made a mistake and it should have been a left turn. I opened my mouth to blame David when something clicked inside me. What was the point! It would only start an argument. Why not admit I was wrong – which I was. So I did just that. 'Sorry it was my fault. I took a wrong turn,' I said sheepishly. The girls in the back gasped with surprise. David shrugged his shoulders and said calmly, 'That's okay, let's try again.' The reactions were interesting. The girls' shock made me realise what a bad model I had been, and David's calm made me realize that, though I had taken a wrong turn that day, in fact I had just chosen the right direction for happy travelling in the future!

Ability to admit to and apologise for mistakes is important. However, too many errors may still erode a leader's integrity. If he is continually making errors of judgement and poor choices it is not enough to keep apologising.

Eventually his people are going to conclude that he does not possess the qualities that a leader needs. It is a question of aligning one's gifting to the right role. Some are leaders, but only in a certain sphere. For example a person with a teaching gift may have the leadership skills to head up a department in a school, but not the gifts to become the head teacher of the whole school. Or a head teacher may be a good leader in a school but not for pastoring a large church. I once met a pastor who had been a major in the army. He ran his church just as he had run his men – not the best leadership model for a church!

THE SERVANT LEADER

The Bible gives us many examples of good leadership. Moses was a person God spoke to face to face. He was a great leader yet was described as the humblest man on the face of the earth.[20] King David was chosen when still a boy to reign over the people of Israel. He was a brave warrior, a gifted musician and became a great king who left an incredible legacy for his son Solomon to inherit. He was also a man of integrity. We read that he 'shepherded them [the people of Israel] with integrity of heart; with skilful hands he led them.'[21] Nehemiah put his brother Hanani in charge of Jerusalem because he was a man of integrity and feared God more than most men do. Timothy, Paul's protégé, was a young leader that Paul was schooling for more responsibility. Paul encouraged him to watch his life and his doctrine; to persevere in them because if he did he would *save* both himself and his hearers.[22] The word 'save' is from the Greek word *sozo* which means to preserve, save, heal or make whole. Integrity is largely a result of living a life of self-awareness. This is the sort of life Paul wanted Timothy to live because it would bless those he ministered to, as well as himself.

However, Jesus is our supreme example of leadership. He took a motley band of twelve men and for three years lived with them in close proximity. He modelled Christian leadership to them as well as taught it. Just before he died he gave them an example to follow that they would never forget. Certain things are easy to remember. One of these is the last word of a person we love. I remember and treasure the last words of my mother to me the day before she died. I will never forget them. Jesus knew that what he did in those last hours before his crucifixion would be indelibly printed on his disciples' memories. During the last meal he had with them he shocked them by suddenly getting up from the table, taking off his outer garment and tying a towel around his waist. He poured water into a basin and began washing their feet. He was their leader, their teacher, and some believed – their Messiah. How could he stoop so low as to wash feet, a task only servants did? Why did he do it?

He was Challenging the Values of the Culture

The disciples had grown up in the culture of the first century where religious leaders were treated differently from everyone else. They expected people to respect them and honour them by making way for them and giving them the best places wherever they were invited. It was a society where only servants washed the feet of those entering a house after a journey. The dust and dirt would have made this a necessity not a luxury. When Jesus, their leader, began to wash their feet he turned the cultural norms of that era upside down.

Today, in many people's minds, success equals money and fame, our 'rights' come before loving our neighbour, truth is anyone's guess, integrity is outmoded and leaders stand on platforms preaching one thing and doing another. In the upper room Jesus challenged his disciples' concept of leadership, just as today he challenges ours. He says. 'I have set you an example that you should do as I have done for you.'[23] He turns our values upside down, but above all, he challenges our ideas of leadership.

He was Setting Them an Example.

Jesus knew what it was to be tempted by Satan to use his power for his own needs, to glorify himself and to short cut God's will for his life. He knew that down through the ages Satan would try and divert Christian leaders with the same temptations. At this last meal with his disciples Jesus knew that he was about to leave them on their own. They were a bunch of Galilean hillbillies, and they were on the brink of being launched into leading a world movement; a Church that would one day encircle the globe. He knew that it would only survive if it was led by servant leaders. Men and women who were prepared to serve others, take humble roles, and do menial tasks. If they were sidetracked into building their own kingdoms or making great names for themselves, then their world would eventually come crashing down. The seeds of its own destruction would be built into it.

We are told that our attitude should be same as that of Christ Jesus, 'Who, being in the very nature God, did not consider equality with God something to be grasped, but made himself nothing, taking the very nature of a servant.'[24]

The Will of God

John records Jesus' last words from the cross – 'It is finished.' Jesus finished what he set out to do. Isaiah prophesied that the will of God would prosper in Jesus' hands.[25] As he hung on the cross that prophecy was wonderfully and finally fulfilled. Every person aspiring to be a leader would do well to make it his goal – 'That the will of God would prosper in his hands.' But if the goal is to be achieved then a student is not above his teacher and the way of success will be the same way for us as it was for Jesus.

Jesus was Anointed

At the beginning of his ministry Jesus was anointed by the Holy Spirit. From that moment he depended upon the power and guidance of the Holy Spirit. The Holy Spirit is the active agent of the Trinity who has been sent by the Father to come alongside Christians in the world today. None of us can do without his help. But leaders especially need his continual anointing. It is easy to rely on a past blessing and to be running on empty. We need to be filled every day. John Stott is probably one of the most respected and influential leaders in the Evangelical world today. In his study of Paul's letter to the Ephesians he writes: '"Be filled" is not a tentative proposal, but an authoritative command. We have no more liberty to avoid this responsibility than the many others which surround it in Ephesians. To be filled with the Spirit is obligatory, not optional . . . We have to be "sealed" with the Spirit once and for all; we need to be filled with the Spirit and go on being filled every day and every moment of the day.'[26] People often get hung up by talk of the 'second blessing'. I have found it helpful to answer the question, 'When do I receive the second blessing?' with the reply, 'Between the first and the third' (anon).

Affirmation

At the same time as Jesus was baptised in water and anointed by the Holy Spirit, he received a resounding affirmation from his Heavenly Father. 'And a voice came from heaven: "You are my Son, whom I love; with you I am well pleased."'[27] It was a great beginning for his ministry. One of the big gaps in society today is our lack of good fathering. Many children grow up without the presence of their father, and others with very disinterested fathers who do not appreciate how important they are to their children's lives. The illegitimacy rate in Britain has increased in just ten years from one in eight in 1980 to one in three in 1990, leaving many children fatherless. Yet a study from 'Tomorrow's Men Project' supported by Oxford University and funded by Top Man, picked out youngsters with high self-esteem, happiness and confidence as successful 'can-do kids' and

looked in depth at their parental and social backgrounds.
More than 1,500 boys aged 13 to 19 were surveyed. 'High-
level fathering', it found, 'was much the most important factor in success. More than 90 per cent of boys who felt that
their fathers spent time with them and took an active interest in their progress emerged in the "can-do" category.'[28]

Jesus was fully human, as well as being fully God. In his
humanity he needed the presence of a human father and
God provided one in the person of Joseph. We don't know
when Joseph died, but we know that he cared for Jesus and
protected him as a child. We know too that Jesus modelled
himself on Joseph by becoming a carpenter. However, when
the important moment came to begin his public ministry
Jesus received those special words of affirmation from his
Heavenly Father. Throughout his ministry the relationship
between Jesus and his Father was very special. Every leader
needs to enjoy that intimacy with God. He needs to have
the experience of God affirming him. But above all, he
needs to know that he is a chosen and beloved child of the
Living God. The sort of childhood he experienced, his parenting, his education, his success and failure, and the opinions of others, all belong in 'clock time'. But the experience
we have of God is from eternity. A leader might not have
had a very good experience of being parented, but that lack
will only be significant if he has not yet experienced the
affirming love of his heavenly Father. A person who has an
intimate relationship with God will be able to survive the
disappointments and temptations of the ministry, and the
will of God will prosper in such a person's hands.

Jesus chose to Build God's Kingdom – not his own

The will of God is like an entrustment. It is something
which he has entrusted to us. In their teens two of our
daughters came back to school in England from Chile.
Some friends offered to be their guardians. We entrusted
our friends with two of our most precious possessions.

Likewise God has entrusted his precious will to us. Leadership is a very special part of this entrustment. But with every entrustment comes enticement. We have an enemy who seeks to divert us from the will of God, as he did Jesus. Satan offered Jesus the kingdoms of the world if he would only bow down and worship him.[29] Jesus refused to be tempted into building an empire for himself. He set his energies into extending God's kingdom, and he taught his disciples to pray: 'Thy kingdom come.'

Enticements will come! And the enemy knows how to fashion the temptation to fit the individual. For some it will be for applause and approval. It was said of the Pharisees that they loved the praise of men more than the praise from God.[30] I remember once receiving a letter from a prison chaplain. He wrote: 'What people think of me and how they react to me determines my mood for the day . . . I am always wanting people's approval.' He ministered to prisoners but actually was a prisoner himself to other people's opinions. If this is our weakness then our motives will be contaminated by that need.

Another enticement that is especially tailored to those with a low self-image, is to think that position and success will be the cure-all. They believe mistakenly that becoming a 'somebody' will prevent them feeling like a 'nobody'. Building one's own kingdom happens insidiously, almost without noticing. It starts as something good, perhaps a gift for prophecy or preaching. Then it begins to feed the leader's image and to give him a sense of kudos, so the gift subtly changes and becomes something for the person instead of something for God's glory.

Jesus Paid the Price so that God's Will could Prosper

The cost for Jesus was enormous, more than we could ever imagine or comprehend, but the same is true for all his disciples. There is a price to pay. We may not be called to die but we will be asked to die to our own self-centred agendas.

It hurts to say 'no' to sin when we know it would gratify an aching need within. It is painful to sacrifice popularity for the sake of truth, a position for the sake of integrity. It is costly to go the second mile, to turn the other cheek, to love the unlovely as Mother Theresa did.

I remember hearing the story of an elderly Mapuche Indian woman who became sick with cancer of the stomach. A Chilean Christian who lived nearby heard the poor woman was sick and took her some soup. She saw that the old lady was alone and had no one to care for her so she moved in to live with her and look after her. She fed her small spoons of broth all through the night and slept in her bed beside her to keep her warm. Gradually the old lady began to improve and was eventually healed. To appreciate this story one has to understand that the Indians of Chile are looked down on, and in many cases despised, by the Chilean population. It must have been very sacrificial to have loved the old Indian in the way she did. But she paid the price and the will of God prospered.

C. S. Lewis once said: 'There are two kinds of people in the end: those who say to God, "Thy will be done", and those to whom God says, in the end, "Thy will be done."'[31] Standing near the cross John heard Jesus utter those dying words: 'It is finished.' His life's goal had been to do the will of God, and he drew his last breath certain that he had done it. Our commitment to integrity ensures we pursue the same goal.

NOTES

Introduction
1   Matt. 7:3–5

Chapter 1
1   J. Richard Middleton and Brian J. Walsh, *Truth Is Stranger Than It Used To Be* (London: SPCK, 1995) pp19,20.
2   Ibid.
3   Ibid. p25.
4   Os Guinness, *Time for Truth* (Nottingham: IVP, 2000) p12.
5   Ibid. p64.
6   Ibid. p65.
7   Ibid. p12.
8   Ibid. pp26–27.
9   Ibid. p14.
10 Jn. 8:32.
11 Gen. 3:4.
12 Jn. 14:6.
13 Jn. 18:37–38.
14 Eph. 4:25; Matt. 5:37.
15 Guinness, op. cit. p20.

Chapter Two
1   Jer. 17:9.
2   Daniel Goleman, *Vital Lies, Simple Truths* (London: Bloomsbury Publishing plc, 1997) p12.
3   Ibid. p11.
4   Ibid. p12.
5   Richard Dortch, *Integrity: How I Lost It and My Journey Back* (Green Forest, New Leaf Press, 1991) pp56, 312.
6   Goleman, op. cit. p13.
7   Ps. 139:23–24 (*Living Bible*).
8   1 Jn. 1:7.
9   M Scott Peck, *People of the Lie* (New York: Simon & Schuster, 1983) p57.
10 Ibid. p76.
11 Mary Pytches, *Set My People Free* (London: Hodder and Stoughton,

1987) p20.

12 Mitch Alborn, *Tuesdays With Morrie* (London: Doubleday, 1997) pp33, 175.

13 2 Sam. 15.

14 Mary Pytches, *A Child No More* (London: Hodder and Stoughton, 1991) p104.

15 Ps. 51:6.

16 M. Scott Peck, *The Road Less Travelled* (New York: Simon & Schuster, 1978) p51.

Chapter Three

1 Richard F. Lovelace, *Dynamics of Spiritual Life* (Illinois, IVP, 1979) p82.

2 1 Jn.1:7.

3 Phil. 2:19–22.

4 2 Tim. 1:7; 2:1; 1Cor. 16:10; 2 Tim. 2:22.

5 1 Tim. 4:16.

6 Gen. 12:2–3.

7 Gen 15:6.

8 Phil. 2:12–13.

9 Rom. 8:29.

10 Ex. 15:11.

11 Lev. 20:7–8.

12 1 Pet. 1:15.

13 Matt. 5:48.

14 Ps. 31:5; Is. 65:16.

15 Ps. 51:6.

16 Os Guinness, *Time for Truth* (Nottingham: IVP, 2000) p134.

17 Jn. 8:31–32.

18 Jn. 16:13.

19 1 Jn. 4:16.

20 Jn 17:11.

21 Daniel Goleman, *Vital Lies, Simple Truths* (London: Bloomsbury Publishing plc, 1997) p244.

22 Dr Phillip C. McGraw, *Life Strategies* (London: Vermilion, 1999) p114.

23 Ibid. p91.

24 M. Scott Peck, *The Road Less Travelled* (New York: Simon & Schuster, 1978) p61.

25 McGraw, op. cit. p122.
26 Rom. 8:28.
27 Ps. 139:23–24.

Chapter Four

1   Os Guinness, *Time for Truth* (Nottingham: IVP, 2000) p118.
2   Daniel Goleman, *Vital Lies, Simple Truth* (London: Bloomsbury Publishing plc, 1997) p13.
3   Ibid. p122
4   Interview with Emily Sheffield in *Sunday Telegraph Magazine* 28th October 2001.
5   M. Scott Peck, *People of the Lie* (New York: Simon & Schuster, 1983) p138.
6   M. Scott Peck, *Further Along the Road Less Travelled* (New York, Simon & Schuster Ltd, 1993) p51.
7   Goleman, op. cit. p119.
8   Guinness, op. cit. p130.
9   Article by Philip Delves Broughton in *The Daily Telegraph*, (January 2001).
10 Guinness, op. cit. p130.
11 Ibid. p66.
12 Richard Dortch, *Integrity: How I Lost It and My Journey Back* (Green Forest, New Leaf Press, 1991) p128.
13 Ibid. p319.
14 Goleman, op. cit. p121.
15 1 Sam. 23:7.
16 Dortch, op. cit. p313.
17 Article by Richard Savill in *The Daily Telegraph*, 11th October 2001.
18 Dr Laura Schlessinger, *The Ten Commandments* (Cliff Street Books, 1998) p228.

Chapter Five

1   Edmund Burke (1729–1797).
2   Select Letters of John Newton (London: Banner of Truth Trust, 1960) p63.
3   Matt. 5:37.
4   Ibid. p50.
5   Os Guinness, *Time for Truth* (Nottingham: IVP, 2000) p14.

6 Guinness, op. cit. p88.
7 Stephen Covey, *Seven Habits of Highly Effective People* (London: Simon & Schuster, 1992) p197.
8 Jn. 8:32.

Chapter Six
1 Jn. 15:5.
2 Ps. 139:23–24.
3 Dr Phillip C. McGraw, *Life Strategies* (London: Vermilion, 1999) p123.
4 2 Sam. 12.
5 Ps. 51.
6 McGraw, op. cit. p82.

Chapter Seven
1. 1 Chron. 29:17.
2 Rom. 8:28.
3 Jam. 1:2–4.
4 Prov. 27:21.
5 Helena Wilkinson, *Beyond Chaotic Eating* (London: HarperCollins, 1993) p84.
6 Michael Ford, *Wounded Prophet* (London: Darton, Longman and Todd, 1999).
7 Henri Nouwen, *Life of the Beloved* (Hodder and Stoughton, 1992) p39.
8 Matt Redman, *The Unquenchable Worshipper* (East Sussex: Kingsway Communications 2001) pp64–5.
9 Jn. 13:37–38.
10 Matt. 6:5,17.

Chapter Eight
1 Is. 6:5.
2 Is. 6:3.
3 Is. 6:7.
4 Deut. 7:22.
5 Josh. 5:13–6:5.
6 Josh. 10:11–15.
7 Colin Whittaker, *Great Revivals* (Basingstoke: Marshall Morgan and Scott, 1984) p27.

8 Ibid. p31.
9 Brian H. Edwards, *Revival! A People Saturated with God* (Darlington: Evangelical Press, 1990) p187.
10 Ibid. p114.
11 Whittaker, op. cit. p170.
12 Job 38:4,12; 40:7; 42:4.
13 Heb. 12:14.

Chapter Nine

1 Dr Phillip C. McGraw, *Life Strategies* (London: Vermilion, 1999) p134.
2 Stephen R. Covey, *Seven Habits of Highly Effective People* (London: Simon & Schuster, 1992) p46.
3 McGraw, op. cit. p.231.
4 Reginald Johnson, *Your Personality and the Spiritual Life* (East Sussex: Monarch, 1995).
5 Crusade for World Revival.
6 Johnson, op. cit.
7 John Powell, *The Secret of Staying in Love* (Allen, Texas: Tabor Publishing, 1974).
8 Jn. 8:32.
9 C. S. Lewis, *The Four Loves* (London: Collins, 1960) p7.
10 Richard Dortch, *Integrity: How I Lost It and My Journey Back* (Green Forest, New Leaf Press, 1992) p319.

Chapter Ten

1 Os Guinness, *Time for Truth* (Nottingham: IVP, 2000) p133.
2 Matt. 22:16.
3 Stephen Covey, *Seven Habits of Highly Effective People* (London: Simon & Schuster, 1992) p197.
4 M. Scott Peck, *The Road Less Travelled* (New York: Simon & Schuster, 1978) p56.
5 Jn. 3:19.
6 Peck, op. cit. p52.
7 Heb. 10:24.
8 Interview with Erin Brockovich (*Hello* Magazine).
9 Matt. 7:3–5.
10 Matt. 5:8.
11 Prov. 11:3.

12 George New and David Cormack, *Why Did I Do That?* (London: Hodder and Stoughton, 1997) p9.

13 Prov. 20:7 (KJV).

14 Covey, op. cit. p197.

15 Dr Laura Schlessinger, *The Ten Commandments* (New York: Cliff Street Books, 1998) p246.

16 Prov. 10:9.

17 Covey, op. cit. p298.

18 Rom. 8:1.

19 Peck, op. cit. p51.

20 Matt. 6:24: 'No-one can serve two masters. Either he will hate the one and love the other, or he will be devoted to the one and despise the other.'

Chapter Eleven

1 John Maxwell, *Developing the Leader Within You* (Nashville: Thomas Nelson Publishers, 1993) p37.

2 *Scent of a Woman*, Universal Pictures (1993).

3 Anthony Sampson, *Mandela* (London: HarperCollins, 1999) pp583,585.

4 James M. Kouzes, Barry Z. Posner, *Credibility* (Chichester: Jossey-Bass, 1993) p11.

5 Maxwell, op. cit. p35.

6 *Great Quotes from Great Leaders*, ed. Peggy Anderson (New Jersey: Lombard, 1989).

7 Matt. 25:21.

8 1 Kings 3:9.

9 1 Kings 3:16–28.

10 Ex. 28:30.

11 Maxwell, op. cit. p38.

12 Max De Pree, *Leadership Jazz* (New York: Dell Publishing Co., 1992) p60.

13 Maxwell, op. cit. p41.

14 Ibid. p44.

15 De Pree, op. cit. p9.

16 John Maxwell, *Developing the Leaders Around You* (Nashville: Thomas Nelson Publishers, 1995) p132.

17 William J. Bennett, *The Death of Outrage* (New York: Simon & Schuster, 1998) p41.

18 Kouzes & Posner, op. cit. p59.
19 Ibid. p205.
20 Num. 12:3.
21 Ps. 78:72.
22 1 Tim. 4:16.
23 Jn. 13:15.
24 Phil. 2:5–6.
25 Is. 53:10.
26 John R. W. Stott, *God's New Society* (Leicester: IVP, 1979) p208.
27 Lk. 3:22.
28 Article by Mark Henderson, *The Times* (28th January 1999).
29 Matt. 4:8.
30 Jn. 12:43.
31 C. S. Lewis, *The Great Divorce* (Glasgow: Collins) p66.